ROLEPLAYING IN BUSINESS AND INDUSTRY

Roleplaying
IN BUSINESS AND INDUSTRY

Raymond J. Corsini
INDUSTRIAL RELATIONS CENTER,
UNIVERSITY OF CHICAGO
ASSOCIATE DIRECTOR, DANIEL D. HOWARD ASSOCIATES

Malcolm E. Shaw
VISITING LECTURER, CORNELL UNIVERSITY
DIRECTOR, MALCOLM SHAW ASSOCIATES

Robert R. Blake
PROFESSOR OF PSYCHOLOGY, UNIVERSITY OF TEXAS
DIRECTOR, HUMAN RELATIONS TRAINING LABORATORY

The Free Press of Glencoe, Inc.
A DIVISION OF THE CROWELL-COLLIER PUBLISHING COMPANY

To Dr. J. L. Moreno

OUR MUTUAL FRIEND, COUNSELOR, AND TEACHER

Foreword

THE HARD CORE of any enterprise is the relationship between the leaders and the led. In the unceasing struggle of life, be it the individual who seeks to improve himself, the company that tries to grow or the nation that seeks greatness, the answer for advancement and survival depends on doing things better, simpler, and easier.

In any group enterprise, success is a function of good leadership. It is the most priceless commodity in any society. Good leaders of men are born and they are made. Regardless of one's talents in this direction, improvement in leadership potential is a function of training—be it by books, by experience, or by observation.

Probably the most crucial question we can ask in this area is: "Are we learning leadership skills fast enough?" I think not. Practical psychology has been dangerously surpassed by technological skills. I see no more serious problem in the world today than the location and nurture of our most precious vital resource—creative leadership.

Of the many techniques for self, and other, improvement ranging from reading through experience, none is more rapid,

v

more useful, more dramatically effective than roleplaying for many purposes, but especially for the inculcation of human relations skills. Although roleplaying has been used fairly effectively by isolated personnel men and industrial trainers, to date there has been lacking a single unified and complete presentation of what to do in roleplaying and how to do it.

Roleplaying in Business and Industry meets this need effectively. Simple and direct in its style, comprehensive and authoritative, it is the joint product of three of the leading practitioners of roleplaying in this country, men whose sound knowledge of the theory of human behavior is supplemented, as can be seen by the credits on the title page, by practical day-by-day experience in the problems of leadership in business and industry.

Although this is a how-to-do-it-yourself book, training directors, sales managers, and line supervisors will find it valuable in presenting the "why" as well as the "how" and the "what" of roleplaying. Those seeking a comprehensive guide to this fascinating technique will find it in this book.

ROBERT K. BURNS, PH.D.

EXECUTIVE OFFICER, INDUSTRIAL RELATIONS CENTER
UNIVERSITY OF CHICAGO

Acknowledgment

THE AUTHORS wish to thank the following people for their assistance: Dr. Daniel D. Howard and Mrs. Barbara White for critical reading of the manuscript and various suggestions; and Mrs. Sandra Novoselsky for her typing of a complicated manuscript.

Note

THE LETTERS *r-o-l-e-p-l-a-y-i-n-g* represent at least four distinct concepts and have been spelled in two ways: "role playing" and "role-playing." One of the concepts, the central concern of this book, is here spelled "roleplaying" in line with the general tendency in the English language for associated words to be first hyphenated and then joined. The four concepts are:

1. *Theatrical.* In this sense an actor plays a role as defined by the playwright and the director. The actor repeats over and over certain words and actions in a predetermined manner.

2. *Sociological.* This concept refers to the usual behavior of people in particular societies, how they act under certain circumstances in formal ways; it has been used in the sense that all social behavior represents a playing of culturally determined patterns.

3. *Dissimulative.* In this sense people play roles with the intention of deceiving, or of creating impressions contrary to their real feelings. The spy in enemy territory or the employe who is polite to a disliked superior are playing roles.

4. *Educational.* In this concept, the subject of this book, roleplaying is an action-spontaneity procedure which takes place under contrived circumstances. It has three general classes of purposes: (a) Diagnostic—to provide better understanding of the roleplayers by seeing and hearing them in action, (b) Informative—to give the auditors and spectators information how certain roles should be filled, and (c) Training—to provide the roleplayers with knowledge and skills by permitting them to experience a near-veridical situation, and to understand themselves and their behavior better through feedback information.

Contents

Introduction

THAT A SERIOUS BOOK about business and industry should be concerned with "playing" requires a bit of explanation. Everyone knows complicated skills have to be learned, and that such learning calls for a good deal of practice. The young surgeon, for example, has many years of training, and before he can operate must observe other surgeons and serve a long apprenticeship. The concert pianist rehearses for many weary hours before he appears on the stage. Baseball players have their spring practice. But where can one learn those complicated and all-important human relations skills of leading, managing, and co-ordinating people? One answer is in industry itself; and one method is "roleplaying."

Roleplaying has been called "reality make believe," "reality practice," "sensitivity training" and "action learning." It involves realistic behavior under unrealistic conditions. The boxer who spars with his shadow is roleplaying; the lawyer who argues a case before his family is roleplaying; the executive who practices his speech on his stenographer is roleplaying. These people are "making believe" that what they are doing is "for real" even though they—and others—know that it is only "practice."

Why, one may ask, need one roleplay? Cannot one learn through reading books or through listening to lectures or by watching films? Yes: but roleplaying is a much more effective manner of learning complex skills because it is "learning through doing." In roleplaying one thinks, feels and acts at the same time: one is involved comprehensively and globally in the situation. Too often in life we know what to do but cannot do it, either because of fear or other emotional complications or because we just don't have the skills. There is no difference in essence between learning to fly an airplane or handling a labor dispute: both may be learned by watching others, through lectures and by books, but it is only through experience that one can really learn to do any job adequately. Roleplaying provides a simulated reality experience in which one can practice complex skills without hurting himself or anyone else through failure.

Roleplaying has many purposes, and in this book some of its uses will be discussed. It is possible to classify the specific purposes under three general headings: Training, Informing, and Testing.

Training. All procedures with the objective of improving skills may be called training. For example, if a new salesman roleplays a tough selling situation and the purpose is to enable him to actually meet a tough situation in real life, this is training. He is "learning by doing."

Informing. When trainees are watching and listening and not roleplaying themselves, roleplaying is then used for informing, and the roleplayers become living audio-visual devices.

Testing. When the purpose of roleplaying is to analyze and evaluate the roleplayer, then the procedure is done for testing purposes.

Purpose of the Book

This book is intended to serve as an introduction and manual to roleplaying. It is directed to line and staff people in business and industry concerned with the development of personnel in human relations areas: selling, interviewing, handling grievances and disputes, co-ordinating work, supervising, etc. While much of this material is useful for those who may use roleplaying in other connections: in education, counseling, community affairs, etc., our emphasis is on commercial enterprises, where roleplaying has already been used with good results.

The three authors have assumed various responsibilities for parts of the book, but it is a collaboration, since each part has been read, revised, edited, and approved by all three. Since we have considerably different experiences and points of view in this field, the reader may be reassured that he will not be presented with a single partisan picture but rather with the consensus of our thinking.

Blake was responsible for the first section, *Background.* This section contains the history, theory, and general implications of roleplaying. This section should provide a relatively complete frame of reference for understanding the meaning and purpose of roleplaying.

The second section, *Techniques,* written by Corsini, deals with a variety of action roleplaying procedures. It should help the beginner know how to proceed and what to guard against in roleplaying.

The third section, *Applications,* was the responsibility of Shaw. This part concerns itself with the various uses of roleplaying. It explains how and for what purposes roleplaying may be used.

The fourth section, prepared by Corsini, consists of structured situations which the beginning roleplaying director can use in developing himself. An annotated bibliography of roleplaying in industry and allied areas, a glossary, and observer recording forms are also found in this section.

We hope the reader will use this volume as a springboard for creative roleplaying. Like the interview, roleplaying is a simple technique whose possibilities no one shall ever master completely. We believe it has exciting, profitable, potentialities. No industrial leader should be without a basic understanding of the meaning, purposes, values, and potentialities of roleplaying. If we have been of help in pointing out what roleplaying can be used for, our efforts are well repaid.

RAYMOND J. CORSINI
MALCOLM E. SHAW
ROBERT R. BLAKE

BACKGROUND

The Human Equation
in Business and Industry

IN BUSINESS AND INDUSTRY *people* run machines, perform services, make sales. They create, design, plan, supervise, direct, evaluate, decide, reward, and punish. Machines, work methods, technical processes, and so on *are* important, but decisions regarding work itself are made with, through, and by people.

People involved in work processes ought to give top effort toward the success of the enterprise. That's what they're paid to do. But what are the facts? Sometimes the situation and the people "click." Everything goes right. Frequently, though, things don't work out. Morale is low. People become apathetic, frustrated, and competitive. They gripe and put up with their jobs to get the *other* things a salary makes possible. Conflict, low morale, disinterest, antagonism, resistance, absenteeism, inefficiency, and turnover are signs that something in the human dimension is out of kilter. Somewhere along the line, human mistakes are being made that dissipate involvement, enthusiasm, initiative, creativity, and happiness.

6

Modern industry is faced with a herculean task on the human side of the enterprise. How may we employ people more effectively than at present?

There are four possible alternatives for viewing this problem.

1. *Disregard the fact that people have difficulties with one another.* Take the attitude that human difficulties are inevitable, "Human nature being what it is . . . ." Argue that problems between people can't be avoided, so they must be lived with.

2. *Hope problems will disappear.* This is a blind hope that never has paid off; the same old problems are always with us.

3. *Try to solve human problems through increased pay and other forms of reward.* The last decade has shown that pay as an incentive is weakly related to productivity, to creativity, or to work satisfaction. Human problems continue to exist in spite of increases in wages.

4. *Search for and develop solutions to human problems.* It is in this alternative that the promise of the future lies. People *can* learn to avoid making human blunders. Many procedures are possible to aid in the wiser use of human resources.

Some Common Solutions

To meet and to solve human problems, industry has employed a number of procedures. The *interview* is used to select, instruct, advise, criticize, correct, and appraise. The *lecture* is employed to announce, inform, and instruct. The *conference,* for board and staff meetings, training sessions, safety meetings, etc. is becoming increasingly popular. Many organizations use *publications* to aid in distributing information, building morale, instructing, controlling, etc. *On-the-job training*, with observation, lectures, and guided instruction, is used for teaching new skills. *Rotation* acquaints and broadens an individual's outlook and understanding beyond the limits of his present job. For evaluation purposes, including selection, decisions about training, upgrading, and transferring, *tests and questionnaires* of many varieties, standard and projective, are used.

Despite these procedures human problems remain. The search continues for more effective approaches to problems on the human side of the enterprise.

Roleplaying

In recent years a new method for *all of the above purposes* has come into prominence. This procedure is known under the general name of *roleplaying*. It has also been called "action training," "sensitivity training," "practicing management," or "action development." Despite its novelty and complexity, it has impressed many people in business and industry with its potentialities. Roleplaying is also being used in psychotherapy and education (27).

A Definition

Roleplaying may be defined as a method of human interaction that involves realistic behavior in imaginary situations. It is a "spontaneous" technique, since participants act freely rather than from a script. It is a "make believe" kind of situation, where people act as though what they were doing was "for real." It uses are many and will be discussed in greater detail later. The major purposes of industrial roleplaying are the instruction and evaluation of managerial personnel, providing insights into the nature of human behavior, and training for requisite skills in dealing with various human situations.

Origins

There is no record of the origins of industrial roleplaying. Probably they go back to the first time an employer said to his apprentice: "Make believe I am a customer, and show how you would treat me." The apprentice acted his own role. The employer acted the role of the imaginary customer. If they stopped now and then and discussed, evaluated, and practiced alternative ways of reacting, they *roleplayed*.

A Viennese psychiatrist, J. L. Moreno, is the originator of the modern concepts of roleplaying and is a strong proponent of spontaneous action methods for psychotherapeutic purposes. He employs a complex version of roleplaying, known as *psychodrama*. From his writings, the rationale and methods of industrial roleplaying may be understood. Moreno's use of roleplaying, dates from about 1923.[1] Moreno maintains that emotional problems can be corrected if people act out troubling situations and analyze and practice new solutions.

Another independent beginning goes back to about 1933. The German Army, limited to 100,000 men by the terms of the Versailles Treaty, began to develop a corps of officers. For the selection of military personnel, Simoneit, a German military psychologist, devised a number of action procedures very similar to current roleplaying in which higher officers could estimate the qualities of army recruits, for effective selection.[2] After the fall of Dunkirk, the British Army employed similar procedures in its officer selection program.[3] In the United States, the Office of Strategic Services used roleplaying for the selection of people for secret war time work.[4]

---

1. J. L. Moreno, *Das Stegreif Theater*. Potsdam: Kiepenhever, 1923.
2. M. Simoneit, *Wehr Psychologie*, Charlottenberg: Bernard & Graefe, 1933.
3. A. Tegla Davies, *Industrial training*, London: Institute of Personnel Management, 1956.
4. O.S.S. Assessment Staff. *Assessment of men*. New York: Rinehart & Co., 1948.

Roleplaying began to be used in the United States for industrial purposes during and immediately after World War II, with early reports of its use in industrial training by Lippitt in 1943 (44) and by French in 1945 (33). More recent general statements of roleplaying in industry are by Argyris (8) and Corsini (24).

At the current time roleplaying has been accepted as a valuable procedure in many industrial organizations. In justice to the procedure, however, it must be said that there are relatively few individuals in industry at the present time who have either the understanding or skill to use roleplaying to anything near its true and full potentialities. Wilkinson and Myers have discussed this matter in some detail (99).

Applications

Evaluation

Business depends on accurate evaluations for personnel selection, analyzing training needs, determining operational changes, and so on. When it comes to human relations situations or problems, it is often hard to get valid or reliable information. Roleplaying can be of considerable value for this purpose. This procedure gives supervisors a chance to see and hear a person in action in a simulated but psychologically real situation.

Example. A candidate for the job of door-to-door salesman is asked to roleplay a typical selling situation. The purpose is to evaluate the candidate's ability to do this work adequately. This kind of roleplaying is a "test." It provides a sample of the candidate's ability to fill a particular position.

Roleplaying also can be used to determine effective or ineffective ways of handling certain operations or assignments.

10

Example. Three people in a personnel department do the same kind of interviewing. Brown typically interviews seven people a day, Jones, eleven, and Smith, fifteen. Each seems to do an equally good job with applicants. Their supervisor would like to bring Brown and Jones up to Smith's level of efficiency. To do so, he would like to find out what typical procedures are used by each of the three men.

One method might be direct observation of each of the men while they are interviewing. This may be unwise, since it can change the relationship between the interviewer and the interviewee. A more practical method is to have Brown, Jones, and Smith roleplay an interviewing situation. The observers may use a checklist to evaluate each man as he roleplays. If Smith maintains his efficiency over Brown and Jones in the roleplaying tests, the other two might be asked to evaluate Smith's methods and then try to make use of them.

Brown and Jones may use procedures in interviewing not useful or necessary. Brown, for example, may spend a good deal of time trying to establish rapport with the interviewee. Smith may proceed directly to the business at hand. Through roleplaying, the performance of each interviewer can be evaluated with inefficiencies spotted and eliminated.

Roleplaying may also be used for evaluating and improving supervisory practices.

Example. In a particular department morale is low, and the source of the low morale is evidently the foreman. He is interested in finding out what causes his troubles. Before observers he roleplays typical situations he meets on the job. Through discussions with those who observe him roleplaying, he comes to recognize what is ineffective in his approach to employees.

Roleplaying may be used for numerous other types of evaluation. It has an advantage over alternative procedures (questionnaires, tests, interviews, data sheets, etc.) in that it is *here and now, natural* and *spontaneous.* It provides observers with direct material, pertinent to the evaluation, not distorted by errors in communication common to other procedures. Borgatta who investigated the relative value of diagnostic tests and roleplaying reported roleplaying to be more accurate than paper and pencil tests for the prediction of human behavior (16).

Training

Perhaps the most important use of roleplaying is for training. It provides a person practice in a particular job so that he can learn the new skills needed to do it adequately.

Example. A man has been hired as a door-to-door salesman. He has no previous experience in this type of selling. A roleplaying situation in which a salesman calls on a housewife is set up and the new man plays the role of salesman. By this make-believe, by discussing and evaluating his performance and then by trying out other ways of doing it, the new man gets training and practice in the skills of salesmanship.

For improving skills in a particular job, a variety of roleplaying situations may be set up. For example, an individual may demonstrate how he handles a certain situation. Discussion and analysis follow, including suggestions from the leader and the group as to how the performance may be improved. The trainee may try the role again making an effort to vary his procedure. He may watch others as they demonstrate how they handle the role.

Example. A salesman is in a slump; sales have been falling off. Advice and encouragement have not helped him. A roleplaying situation is set up, involving a salesman and a prospective customer. The salesman plays his own role. He runs through the roleplaying scene several times. Observers tell him that he acts hesitantly and seems ill at ease. Perhaps the salesman cannot believe this is so. Someone else then acts out the role as he saw the salesman act it. The salesman protests that this portrayal is a crude distortion of how he himself played the role, but the others may assure him that the portrayal was correct. They also demonstrate other approaches for him to try. He then re-enacts the role and tries to handle it in a different way. Or he might even play the part of the prospective customer while someone else plays his role.

Roleplaying is well suited for training in human relations skills. It helps increase understanding of other people, and it gives insight into the skills necessary for dealing with interpersonal situations. Any job that involves human interaction can be approached through roleplaying. The foreman, the supervisor, the plant superintendent, the sales manager, the physician, the receptionist—each has to deal with people. In each of these positions, how one deals with others is often crucial for success.

Instruction

Instruction is the transmission of information from one source to another. The most usual method of live instruction is the lecture. Educators have learned that visual aids such as films, slides, and posters help maintain interest and improve communication. A message is more likely to be understood and retained if it is dramatic. The good lecturer makes his message forceful by gestures, changes in tone, rhetorical questions, and so on. It is effective if the audience can *see* what is being discussed—and better still—*see and hear it*. Roleplaying, since it is a dramatic situation, arouses interest, holds attention, and thus helps to implant messages firmly.

Example. A salesman is to be trained in the techniques of selling. He may watch two experienced salesmen enact a number of selling situations. One takes the part of the salesman; the other takes the part of the prospective customer. At one time the prospect may be hostile; at another time he may be luke-warm; a third time he may be eager. The new salesman sees and hears how experienced salesmen handle each of these situations.

When a group is to be instructed, those who do the role-playing need not be acting something important to them. They are actors, putting on a spontaneous drama focused on a particular problem. The effect depends on the meaningfulness of the drama to audience members.

Example. The management of a company has decided on a policy change that will affect all employees. Management feels it essential that foremen understand the reasons for the change so they can interpret it correctly to their employees.

A meeting is called to inform the foremen of these reasons. The leader has several people sit around a table who act the part of management while the foremen look on. Their discussion concerns the policy change, and they debate the pros and cons. The foremen thus witness a vivid portrayal of the reasons for the change. Roleplayers then discuss how employees will react to the change. They predict a negative attitude and decide that foremen must be convinced of the importance of this new policy.

Two people are then called on to play the roles of an executive and a foreman. The "foreman" and the "executive" discuss the change in policy. Then the same "foreman" talks

14

to some "employees," and these "employees" raise objections to the change. The "foreman" finally convinces them of its value.

In this manner, the *real* foremen in the audience become instructed about the problem in a dramatic manner. They hear the objections which employees raise. More important, they witness the way in which they as foremen may be able to meet and overcome objections.

Using roleplaying for instructional purposes, then, is of value particularly when changes in attitude and behavior are desired. Shaw has given examples and evaluated roleplaying as an approach to job instruction (75).

Increased Understanding and Changing Behavior

Roleplaying is particularly effective in helping people to understand others. When we play the role of some other person, we literally put ourselves in his place. We try to feel and behave as he would. If we succeed, roleplaying has increased our understanding of him.

Roleplaying is also helpful in bringing about changes in behavior. It is well known that there can be a discrepancy between one's knowledge and one's behavior. Old habits are resistant to change. A foreman may be told that the use of sarcasm is a poor technique for dealing with employees. He may even accept this idea. But, in spite of "knowing better," he continues to use the old technique. If he takes part in a roleplaying situation with his usual sarcasm and becomes aware of its effects on others, however, he may then learn to avoid such behavior. Or if he watches another person act and talk as he himself usually does, the effects of sarcasm may be vividly impressed upon him. The possibility of change and improved behavior is thus much increased.

15

Summary

Personnel problems in industrial organizations are evidenced by conflict, low morale, frustration, and turnover. The interview, the conference, various kinds of publications, on-the-job-training, rotation, and testing programs are methods used to deal with these problems. Another method is role-playing, which is spontaneous human interaction involving realistic behavior in imaginary situations for purposes of training, instructing, or evaluating. It has come into prominence in industry in the past decade. Typical examples of applications of roleplaying have been provided. The next chapter explores the theory of learning on which roleplaying is based.

Rationale of Roleplaying

TO UNDERSTAND roleplaying's particular advantages for evaluation, training, and instruction, a clear idea of its underlying rationale is necessary. By stepping away from the industrial scene we may examine different approaches currently used for the solution of interpersonal problems which can aid us in formulating a more precise rationale of roleplaying.

At the present time there are three distinct approaches to teaching how to deal more effectively with people. One is *lecturing*—as in the classroom. Another is *interviewing*—as in counseling and psychotherapy. A third is *roleplaying*.

Lecture Methods

In the typical classroom the teacher stands before students who face him, seated in chairs bolted to the floor, or nailed together in rows. The teacher often follows an outline. Notepads opened and pencils ready, the students summarize what the teacher says. Occasionally a question may be asked and answered. Learning is measured by examination. This procedure, more or less typical of traditional classroom teaching, involves a relatively active teacher and passive audience.

Variants of this basic method, using discussion to increase involvement or cases to stimulate problem solving, rest on a similar conception of teaching and are frequently used in industrial training. This classroom method of instruction can be called the "empty container" theory. Students come to the learning situation with receptive but empty minds. The instructor knows what they should learn. His task is to present material in an understandable way and, through examinations, to assess the learning which takes place for each individual. To improve the quality of his teaching, the instructor may use a number of aids. One is a textbook. What he lectures on is amplified in it. Another aid is the blackboard. If a concept can be diagrammed and relationships seen in visual terms, understanding is likely to be improved. A third is the use of audio-visual aids employed to clarify or to dramatize important points. The teacher may assign problems as homework, so that the student applies his learning in a constructive way.

For certain types of subject matter this method constitutes an excellent approach to teaching. When it comes to learning to deal with people, the lecture, by itself, contributes little toward helping an individual to be more effective. Knowledge and verbal insight are insufficient to produce changes in individual behavior.

If formal classroom instruction is inadequate for learning to deal more effectively with people-type problems, then it might be contended that it is necessary to focus on individuals to help them to learn how to behave in an effective manner.

The Interview

Emphasis in individual counseling is not mainly on giving information, but rather on clarifying emotions, feelings, and attitudes. Counseling is a way of stimulating changes in personal behavior. It is a method for repairing personality. Some people in work situations suffer personal problems of an extreme character. For them psychotherapy is the most hopeful answer. Therapeutic roleplaying, however, has been used by Peters and Phelan with industrial supervisors with some success (65).

But individual interviews are no answer to the full spectrum of problems of people working together. There are many reasons why. One reason is that the normal range of human problems in industry is not so "deep" as to require treatment. Personality is only one cause of interpersonal problems and in many situations it is a relatively unimportant consideration. Another reason is that treatment fails in aiding individuals to accommodate to one another successfully when the difficulty stems from factors within the situation itself. An example will serve to clarify this point. The bickering that goes on in many companies between Research and Development and Production is often cleared up merely by exploring the properties of the situation that make for competitiveness and disagreement. Through evaluating the specific feelings experienced by those who are facing the problem, a practical solution is not likely to be found. The effort to treat hostile individuals in order to render them more friendly and co-operative might miss the point that the problem may be in the situation itself. A classroom lecture on problems of intergroup conflict also would probably make little contribution to solving the problem.

The lecture method and the interview constitute two approaches to learning and behavior change. Each method has merit under certain specialized conditions. Both approaches have proven relatively unsuccessful when employed for the purpose of improving relationships between people.

Roleplaying

A human being is complex. He thinks, feels and acts at the same time. He may not have the three in focus: he may think one thing, say another, and feel a third. The most effective manner to reach him, to communicate with him, or to teach him requires that we deal with him as a totality—a thinking, feeling, behaving individual. It is precisely this that roleplaying accomplishes. Roleplaying resembles life more closely than the other procedures.

These questions arise: (1) What aspects of a learning situation help an individual examine his own behavior as a whole and practice methods of changing it? (2) How does roleplaying as a procedure for dealing with human problems meet the requirements of an adequate learning situation?

Emphasis on Personal Problems

An effective learning situation engages a person in actual behavior. How does one act when confronted with problems which are meaningful and personally significant to him? How can he act differently? If the subject matter being studied is *an individual's own behavior*, he must accept the learning situation as relevant to his needs. Thus, he is motivated to study, to inquire, and to experiment. He can relate insights obtained to his actual way of behaving in concrete work situations.

As decribed by Bradford (17), roleplaying creates an active approach to personally meaningful and significant problems. Rarely is this true for lectures, films, or case studies, taken by themselves. Though lectures, films, or case studies may be employed to supplement and reinforce personal-type learning, these procedures usually are too abstract, too general, or too much focused on problems of the typical or hypothetical

20

person to meet training, instructing and evaluating needs in concrete situations. Roleplaying satisfies the requirement that the learning situation be centered on personal, meaningful experiences.

Study of "Normal" Problems

Roleplaying is adapted to investigating normal, everyday, problems; its use is not restricted to "sickness" or personal malfunctioning of a "disturbed" sort. It is useful in studying problems arising from an individual having only a partial view of the situation; from failure of communication to be full and open; from the fact that feelings, attitudes, and legitimate concerns of others are being overlooked, ignored, or misunderstood; from a lack of understanding of time pressures which require decisions to be taken without sufficient opportunity for discussion; from unclear goals, overly autocratic leadership, and so on. These are the common causes of human problems of industry. To be solved they must be approached in an active, concrete, and meaningful way in terms of the person and the situation in which he is functioning.

Active Participation

A unique facet of roleplaying is "active participation in the situation." The person himself has an opportunity to "do," to act in the situation on his own terms. In the traditional classroom situation the student may learn "right" answers, but he gains little or no understanding or capacity to apply them. Learning is too likely to be rote or "by the rule." Ideas don't get into his "muscles." They don't become second nature. Active participation which involves a person testing his own understanding of a problem and trying new ways of solving does contribute to making learning practical and useful.

21

The criticism of "little active participation" applies to lectures and also to films and other kinds of visual aids used for instructional purposes. None, as routinely used, provides an individual with the opportunity of becoming actively engaged with the problem itself. A method is needed which gets the individual closer to the heart of the problem he is trying to understand. Roleplaying provides the individual with the opportunity for active participation in the subject matter being studied through analyzing, exploring, experimenting, and actually trying out new solutions.

Participation with Feedback and Practice

While active participation is a hallmark of an approach to training "that can make a difference," in and of itself, mere participation is not a sufficient condition of learning. The school of hard knocks is centered on participation and personal experience, yet this is a hard, slow, costly road to learning. Frequently it is a very poor way of gaining insight or skill. Participation by itself may mean no more than a lifetime of repeating the same mistakes!

The critical question is whether or not one learns from his participation more about himself, about others, and about the nature of the situation with which he is confronted. Does participation provide opportunity for "stopping the action," for evaluating one's own performance and for getting feedback from others? Does the trainee listen to and understand reactions by others as to "how he is doing"? Does the learning situation provide a "mirror" through which a person can "see" his own behavior? Does it help him to hear how he sounds to other people? Does he listen to what he is being told when others talk with him? If participation lacks these elements, the chances are that the procedure is not of much value. Where

22

it is possible to "stop the action" here and there for evaluation and practice, greater possibilities of learning about one's own behavior arise.

Stopping a sequence of actions to evaluate and to practice alternative modes of reacting is a time-tested method of helping a person learn. Successful coaches use this method in developing tennis players, football teams, golfers, and swimmers. A successful coach may teach out of a book, but he doesn't stop there. He places the student in the actual situation and provides him with an opportunity to test himself. But he doesn't stop there either. He works with the person and helps him to identify mistakes. He provides new practice opportunities so that rehearsal of alternative ways of reacting is possible. The model of a coach working with a player is much closer to real teaching when the subject matter involves human reactions than the model of a teacher lecturing to a group of students, or a father engaged with his son in a "man-to-man" talk.

Essential for instruction based on participation is the use of feedback. Feedback means what the word says: others tell an individual how his behavior appears to them, or he discovers how others were affected by his behavior. Feedback, a basic approach to studying human problems, helps an individual to identify his blind spots and to perceive the kind of information he ordinarily fails to see or hear. By checking his perceptions against those of others, an individual has a measuring rod that helps evaluate his own behavior as well as the behavior of others. By exploring alternative ways of behaving under feedback conditions it is possible to evaluate a variety of possible ways of dealing with a problem. By practicing various kinds of reactions one can become more comfortable in acting in new ways.

23

The Laboratory Analogy to Roleplaying

For a person to learn about his own behavior he must feel free to "expose" his reactions to examination and evaluation by others. Observers in a roleplaying situation help the trainee to identify silent assumptions underlying his conduct, to assess the impact of his behavior on others, and to spot behavioral factors that are sources of difficulty. These gains result in acquisition of increased sensitivity regarding the thoughts and feelings of other people as well as improved self-understanding and superior performance. When an opportunity to experiment with and to practice alternative ways of behaving is provided, real learning leading to behavior changes will occur. Roleplaying provides a person with the opportunity of exploring actual problems under life-like conditions.

Perhaps the analogy to a "laboratory" will place roleplaying in a clearer perspective. If you took a biology course, you might have been provided with a fish, with instructions to dissect it, identify the parts, and then draw a picture of it. Why was this method of instruction employed? The answer is straightforward. Laboratory instruction permitted you to supplement your intellectual understanding of the anatomy of a fish. It gave you the opportunity to feel the fish, to become acquainted with the texture and color of its skin, to experience directly the act of cutting into a fish's body, and of exploring its internal, "under-the-skin" construction. The laboratory instructor, and your laboratory partner, helped you to "know" where to cut, how to handle it, and to identify the various parts, and to spot your mistakes when you got one part confused with another. Then perhaps you were given another specimen and were provided the opportunity of going through the operation again, until you perfected your understanding and technique. By the time you were through, you not only

24

had a better, more concrete knowledge of the structure of a fish, but your attitudes and behavior also had changed. At the outset, perhaps, you didn't like to touch a fish, or you were repelled by the idea of cutting into it. As time went on and your confidence and skill increased, your whole outlook changed. Now you enjoyed exercising your new found understanding and skills. However, a most important consequence resulted from this laboratory experience. You were able to transfer your skills to other activities, they were not restricted in application to the situation within which original learning had taken place. The skills and understanding transferred and generalized to other kinds of specimens.

Was this laboratory experience "playing"? It may have been fun, but it was not "playing." It was serious business, with the definite purpose of helping you to be more skillful in applying your understanding to a concrete, definite object and situation and then of transferring your skills to other situations. The actual work of the laboratory helped you to translate words into action. Were you "playing a role"? Not really. You were simply increasing your ability to act intelligently toward a concrete problem.

An analogy can be drawn between a laboratory exercise in biology and the use of roleplaying to study human problems. In one version of spontaneous roleplaying a situation of personal significance to you is identified. The situation involves a human problem between yourself and another person or other people. The actual other people usually are not present, however. Others "take the roles" of those who are not there but who are involved with you in the actual problem. A problem situation involving you and them is then set out and a typical instance enacted. Others present have an opportunity to observe how you behave and to experience the reactions your behavior produces in them. Because it is a training rather

25

than a work situation, they are free to tell you their reactions to you. You, in turn, can expose your own feelings toward them. Suggestions of more effective ways of dealing with the problem can be explored, with the situation re-enacted to test their adequacy.

On the next occasion, perhaps, you shift your "role" and take the position of the other person with whom you are having difficulty in real life. Now you have the opportunity to explore the situation from *his* point of view. Again the action is halted so that you can describe your thoughts and feelings to others and so that they can react to you. The action starts again and is repeated until you have a more intimate sense of what the real problem is and have had the opportunity to practice various new ways of dealing with it for use in the real situation.

Finally, the problem may be examined from a theoretical and systematic point of view to expand insights regarding the general case, of which the instance under examination is but an example. Now, however, talking about the problem in more general terms is very different from a lecture, because the language is precise and fits actual concrete behavior.

In another version of roleplaying the people who *are involved* in the actual problem may be the participants in a laboratory-type analysis of the kind described. Various additional ways of going about designing a roleplaying session are dealt with in later chapters, as are uses of roleplaying for purposes other than training.

Is this "playing a role"? Not in any literal sense. The words are unfortunate, for they fail to convey the deeper characteristics of the learning situation. If words are disregarded for a moment it can be seen that the approach is very similar to that used in the biology laboratory. The *strategy* of learning in both situations is parallel; the subject matter is different. It is not "playing." It is serious business, undertaken for the definite purpose of helping you to become more skillful in applying your understanding to solve a concrete human problem in a definite situation. Were you "playing a role"? Not really. You may have thought of yourself as the other person, but not seriously. You simply were trying to increase your ability to appreciate the other person's reasons for acting as he does; to act more intelligently by increasing your understanding of how things look and feel from the point of view of another person. You were exploring the properties of a total situation which includes yourself, other people and the context of interaction.

Veridicality

Those who have not personally experienced roleplaying may believe that such acting must be superficial and unreal. Quite the opposite is true: it is a common experience that people, acting roles that are unreal for them will get emotionally involved and will, despite an expectation of acting in an artificial manner, actually begin to behave in a natural manner and will participate intensely and strongly in the situation. The situation becomes "veridical"—psychologically real. Roleplaying is a technique of approaching the study of human problems under laboratory-like conditions. The insights and skills thus learned may have a variety of applications far beyond the specific examples practiced, just as laboratory-based learning in the physical or biological sciences generalizes far beyond the specific examples practiced.

Roleplaying in Human Relations Training

There are several distinctive characteristics of roleplaying as an approach to human relations problems. Perhaps the most

27

distinguishing feature is that training deals with the participants' own concerns. Rather than studying textbook problems, or analyzing a case, or hearing an isolated lecture, or administering a diagnostic test, the training is tailored to the particular needs of the participant himself. The importance of dealing with relevant, personal concerns as emphasized by Bradford (17) is difficult to overestimate.

A second positive feature of roleplaying, as mentioned by Moody (60) and by French (33), is its specific, concrete, active approach. Because people act towards one another globally, roleplaying is able to break through the "verbal barrier," and generates insight and skill where other methods fail. This conclusion is supported in reports by Kaull (40), O'Donnell (63), and Planty (70). The artificial separation between thinking and words on the one hand and action on the other is avoided.

Training for increasing social sensitivity, as described by French (33) and Maier, (50) constitutes a third feature of roleplaying. Moody indicates that the method expands social awareness (60). Frequently, changes in personal attitudes, as mention by Stahl (89), Speroff (79), and Cohen (23) result in increased personal respect for feelings of others. This characteristic of roleplaying stems from the feedback aspect and results from participants being provided information about feelings of others of a kind frequently withheld in work situations. Being more aware of the feelings his behavior evokes in others, an individual is able to adjust his behavior more intelligently and in accordance with the impact it produces on others.

A fourth consideration is that roleplaying provides direct opportunities to practice more skillful ways of relating to others, a value which has been commented on by Stahl (88). The idea of "skill practice" is as appropriate in improving

28

human relationships as in learning to play tennis or to dive.

A final feature is that the *method* employed in roleplaying can be transferred by the person himself to analyze new difficulties in future situations. Not only is an individual learning sensitivity and social skills through roleplaying, he also is learning a novel and constructive way of approaching the analysis and solution of *any* human problem. The latter aspect has been discussed by Blansfield (12).

Theory of Change Applied to Roleplaying

No one has yet provided a completely satisfactory theory to explain the value of roleplaying for the purpose of changing human behavior, although Mead[1] and Moreno[2] have written extensively on the subject.

Moreno has defined spontaneity as "an adequate response to a new situation or a new and adequate response to an old situation." The implications are that in any given human situation a variety of psychological and interpersonal forces are at work. An individual's ability to react successfully to these forces is dependent upon his awareness of them and the freedom with which he can respond once he has become aware. Presumably, we are all inhibited to some extent by our past experience and by a variety of social pressures, which mitigate against free and suitable responses. We might say that people develop established "frozen" patterns of behavior. Frequently these patterns of behavior are not suitable for dealing with immediate problems. Roleplaying is a device for increasing an individual's ability to deal with the "here and now."

A statement by Moreno is pertinent: "When a child first

1. G. H. Mead, *Mind, self and society.* Chicago: University of Chicago Press, 1934.

2. J. L. Moreno, *Who shall survive?* Beacon, New York: Beacon Press, 1953.

begins to become aware of his ability to make sounds he revels in the creative and spontaneous act of experimenting and developing his sound-making facility. He is not concerned with good or bad sounds nor suitable and effective sounds but rather is caught up in the process itself. He soon finds that sounds produce effects and a pattern of sound making begins to develop. He is forced by his parents and society to form sounds into words, etc. Thus, a process which began as an experience in creativity and spontaneity becomes to some extent inhibited and constricted by a variety of pressures and demands. Thus the psychodramatic approach to dealing with functional speech difficulties is to attempt to recreate the spontaneity and creativity in which speech is born. Analogously, roleplaying in interpersonal relations attempts to create a spontaneous and creative setting in which constricting pressures are removed and the individual has an opportunity to learn in a free and uninhibited way."

Thus in Moreno's view one of the crucial factors necessary in roleplaying leading to behavior changes is reduction of inhibitions. Inhibitions prevent a spontaneous and creative expression which means that old behavior forms will be used. Inhibitions must be reduced before changes can occur. What factors prevent creativity and spontaneity? Anticipation of criticism, punishment, and ridicule are all fear producing. Where threats are present an individual is restrained, careful, and conforming. He does not experiment, explore, or try out new modes of acting. Before he is ready to invent, devise, or "play," these fears must be removed. To reduce the roleplayer's anxiety, to get him to become ready to experiment with new forms of human interaction he must "loosen up"—or as the more technical term puts it, he must "warm up." The "warm up" unlocks an individual, because it frees him from doubts and anxieties that his "new" behavior will be criticized, punished, or ridiculed. Through roleplaying, which has the effect of "warming up" participants, constricting pressures preventing consideration and try out of new ways of behaving are removed. Exploration becomes possible. *New* feelings arise. Old feelings are experienced in a new context. Consequences of new behavior can be evaluated. Practice stabilizes this new behavior which can result in real-life changes.

Another approach to understanding the starting and halting, moving forward and then falling backward type of action which is more or less typical of learning through roleplaying is understandable in terms of a theory of change which involves a three-step sequence: (1) frozen behavior, (2) unfreezing, and (3) refreezing. The learning theory enunciated by Lewin[3] is here modified for application to roleplaying.

(1) "Frozen" Behavior

Commonplace, everyday behavior of a kind that an individual can execute "without thinking" is frozen behavior. Greeting a visitor, answering the telephone, instructing a secretary, or conducting a staff meeting in a routine way are examples of frozen behavior. Not too much thought about *approach* or *procedure* is required. Full attention can be placed on the problem being discussed or the topic being analyzed. Under such conditions, adjustments are so automatic that participants are largely unaware of the procedural foundations of their interaction. A result is that the procedural aspects may be inappropriate without the individual having recognition of that fact. An example is when a superior sounds gruff over the telephone. His attitude may not in fact be gruff or rejecting, but he just does not know he appears short and curt in his replies and sharp in his questions. If asked, he says he "just wanted to cut through to the facts," but his way of

3. Kurt Lewin, *Field theory in social science.* New York: Harper, 1951.

cutting through has become so routine that he can't hear himself. He is frozen in a certain typical, stereotyped style of behaving.

Individuals often handle situations with the more or less automatic assumptions characteristic of their approach to any kind of life situation. A result is that standard ways of behaving are proposed and tried. For example, in meetings—use of a chairman and recorder, fixed time intervals for discussion, asking for members who feel opposed to express themselves, the assumption that silence means consent, and so on. But in roleplaying, with feedback evaluations of what's happening, awareness develops that assumptions of an unwarranted character are being made. Emergence into awareness of the existence of stereotypical thinking constitutes a first step toward change. Bradford has emphasized the importance of diagnosis of present behavior in supervisory training (17).

(2) "Unfrozen" Level

An "unfrozen" period follows in social learning through roleplaying. Members become self-consciously aware of their usual approaches and procedural assumptions. Almost every item of behavior stimulates questions and criticism. Counterproposals are made. It seems as though no single way of adjusting will fit the requirements of the situation.

The period of unfreezing is not comfortable. Anxiety is generated when old styles of behavior are labeled "unsatisfactory." The reasons for such tensions are clear, for this represents a period of "unlearning" what already is known but no longer is appropriate. Participants recognize that their own behavior is unsatisfactory, but they have not yet discovered the requirements of more effective action. Eventually new methods are suggested and new procedures tried, until some

32

are identified that do work. This behavior is then refrozen. A new phase then develops.

(3) Refreezing Behavior

A series of phases in the learning cycle can be identified: doing the obvious and typical; "learning" that it doesn't work and the reasons why; trying other things that also don't work; until, finally, new ways of behavior are discovered which are more effective.

There are several ways in which roleplaying leads to more effective problem-solving. Anxiety and disturbances about challenging old ways of behaving lessen as participants learn that unfreezing is necessary for change to take place. The period of unfreezing becomes shorter as experience develops. Members learn to learn. They feel secure about testing a wide range of assumptions, including ones about procedures used in work, in relating to other people, and in searching for alternatives *without* passing through a disturbing unfrozen phase. Such behavior is properly described as flexible, and experimental. To be flexible and experimental, ready to test alternatives, to challenge new solutions for old problems is another way of describing a skilled manager.

The sequence: frozen—unfreezing—refreezing is a way of describing steps in a process of learning. It has application far beyond roleplaying. Modern science, for example, is confronting old, frozen stereotypes regarding products, the way to produce them, and techniques of distribution. In many cases the applications of learning from science have not yet been firmly established. People are unfrozen, dissatisfied with old patterns, but unable to establish new ones. Even organizations undergo periods of being "unfrozen" when they are unable to employ old methods successfully but also uncertain

33

about which new ones to replace them with. Such periods are followed by a refreezing process which becomes the standard way for organizations able to change successfully. Organizations which are flexible and experimental in this sense usually are able to adjust to changing cultural requirements more effectively than organizations which remain untouched by requirements of change and, therefore, persist in their traditional ways. Organizations of the latter kind frequently don't "wake up" until it is too late.

Summary

A rationale of roleplaying has been presented in this chapter by comparing it with lectures and interviews as alternative approaches to understanding and changing behavior. By comparison with these alternative approaches, roleplaying focuses on personal problems which are "normal." It permits active participation, supported by feedback and practice, with freedom for experimentation of the kind made possible by a laboratory kind of atmosphere.

A theory of change based on a three-step cycle of activity from frozen to unfrozen to refrozen behavior is described as the key to the fact that changes occur under roleplaying conditions of a kind unlikely to occur in other approaches to teaching.

Problems of the Human Side of Industry

BEFORE CONSIDERING APPLICATIONS of roleplaying to training, evaluation, and instruction, a question needs to be answered. It is, "What *are* the problems on the human side of the enterprise?" This is an important question because if problems can be identified, then ways can be devised for helping people to deal more effectively with human elements in the business equation.

In answer to this question, 1600 people listed human problems confronted in everyday work situations.[1] These problems can be classified in five major areas:

(a) problems of authority relations.
(b) conducting and participating in meetings.
(c) organizing and handling problems on an intradepartment basis.
(d) managing interdepartmental and intergroup relations.
(e) the over-all design of the organization itself.

1. R. R. Blake and Jane S. Mouton, "*Human relations problem areas in work.*" *Group Psychotherapy,* 1956, 9, 253-264.

These areas indicate the range of human difficulties within industrial life. A better understanding of sources of friction in each of these classes of problem areas can help in evaluating the kinds of treatment most likely to solve them. Examples will be cited to demonstrate the range of problems existing among people in industry. We shall show how roleplaying has been used as a method for dealing with general human relations problems.

Authority Relations

Problems of authority relations appear in all occupational areas. Their commonness indicates the fundamental significance of authority in human interaction. Applications of roleplaying to foreman and supervisory training are furnished by Bradford (17), Bavelas (10), Peters and Phelan (65), Bradford and Lippitt (18), Kellogg (41), and French (33). A text of roleplaying cases containing examples of authority problems is furnished by Maier, Solem, and Maier (52).

Superior-Subordinate

For supervisors one common concern is how to deal with subordinates who are unwilling to accept responsibility. Another concern is with subordinates who are dependent and overdesirous of direction and approval. Such dependency reactions produce complaints by superiors of being interrupted unnecessarily and being required to work at an inappropriate level of detail. Subordinates resistant to accepting necessary direction and guidance are also a source of human relations difficulties. Examples of roleplaying situations depicting this situation are provided by Symonds (94). Resistance to accepting direction is felt mostly by superiors engaged in technical lines of work that require a significant measure of self-direction and personal problem solving by subordinates.

Enforcing rules is another problem area. Superiors often feel enforcement should be unnecessary. Subordinates frequently don't know rules are being violated. Even informal standards such as those regulating coffee breaks, and time out for chit-chats, which subordinates feel are part of the job, may constitute problems for superiors who regard them as a waste of time and as indicating low involvement in their job. Frictions that arise in connection with reprimanding subordinates are related to enforcement. Reprimanding produces feelings of guilt in the superior and feelings of resentment, worthlessness, or defensiveness in the subordinate. The nature of the reprimand may be such that the subordinate's behavior frequently is not altered. Instead, additional problems may arise as a consequence of negative feelings from the reprimand. Roleplaying training in handling grievances is discussed by Shaw (74).

Withholding of information by subordinates creates problems for the superior in obtaining adequate data for use in decision-making. The common assumption made by the subordinate is that giving unfavorable information produces personal criticism or reprisal which can be avoided through withholding it. The superior who evaluates others but has no one to evaluate him faces an unusual set of problems. He becomes isolated. His position removes him from opportunities for "give and take," so that he finds it difficult to see his own position clearly, and to see different ways of proceeding in the execution of his responsibilities.

Applications of roleplaying to supervisory, foreman, and leadership training situations have been reported by American Type Founders Company (2), by Symonds (94) and by Kaull (40).

37

Subordinate-Superior

To the subordinate, problems with superiors are seen in a different perspective. Generally speaking, subordinates report difficulties with superiors who won't change. Zander provides a roleplay description of a situation involving a dominating leader (102), and French of an autocratic leader (32).

One problem has to do with correcting a superior who has inaccurate information. Another is suggesting to a superior a proposal for change in procedure, operation, or direction of work. The problem for the subordinate is to avoid causing the superior to lose status or to avoid being rejected by the superior.

Another problem for subordinates occurs when superiors fail to define limits of authority and responsibility. The boundaries within which the subordinate is free to act independently may be unclear. He doesn't know which actions on his part are likely to produce conflict or criticism. Poorly defined boundaries of authority seem particularly capable of arousing hostility in superiors and anxiety in subordinates. Subordinates required to work without being given sufficient information tend to become tense.

Being unable to discuss problems with a superior because he ends a tension-producing discussion too soon or changes the topic to more neutral content is also a source of friction. When such flight behavior occurs it may frustrate subordinates because real possibilities of altering the disturbing parts of situations are significantly decreased.

Problems with superiors who "pass the buck" are the reverse of those of superiors who criticize subordinates for not accepting responsibility. The superior who is seen as "passing the buck" rather than acting in a responsible manner creates a condition where the subordinate feels prevented from exerting influence in the direction of a desired change. Roleplaying problems of authority relationships involving plagiarism and mutiny are described by Symonds (94).

Evaluation, Appraisal, and Interviewing

Evaluation and appraisal procedures produce interpersonal frictions which appear in remarks characterizing superiors as "unfair," as failing to realize fully the circumstances surrounding a particular complaint or evaluation, or as neglecting to give an adequate explanation of negative components in an appraisal. Appraisals that emphasize personality attributes and fail to give adequate consideration to situational factors in performance are seen by subordinates as inappropriate. This is particularly true when subordinates feel they can change their performance but not their personalities. Subordinates want superiors to take part in setting goals for change which might improve or alter negatively evaluated behavior.

Interviews also constitute a source of human relations difficulties. How to avoid making leading remarks, hearing only what you want to know, feeling uncomfortable when asking personal questions and so on are frequent. Barron (9) and Weinland (98) report on the use of roleplaying in interviewer training for transferring principles into concrete methods of work. Many interviewing-type problems confront sales personnel in contacts with the buying public. Applications of roleplaying in sales training are described by Calhoon (22), Stahl (88), (89), Beckhard (11), and Phelan (69). Examples of interviews involving a hiring situation are reported by Symonds (94). A description of roleplaying for evaluation of participants as clinical psychologist trainees is given by Bronfenbrenner (20).

Conducting Conference, Staff, and Other Meetings

Many problems appear in connection with conducting meetings. Speroff discusses techniques of conducting conference leadership training (84). Training-in-leading conferences are discussed by Massell (55). In a book by Klein (42) is presented a number of problems involving conference leadership and group problem solving from the standpoint of roleplaying. Attitudes of top management toward roleplaying in industry are reported by Marrow (54), a company president.

Chairman or Leader Behavior

Ineffectiveness in decision-making may occur in a chairman's behavior. His failure to recognize the importance of clear and well-formulated goals results in loss of direction. Another important source of stress is found in lethargy and disinterest of members who feel that "in the end he (the department head) will tell us what he wants and how he wants it done." Also included are criticisms of meetings of "report" conferences. Rather than policies being developed within the meeting itself, they are announced, having already been made by the "top brass." The advantage that members become committed, not only to the policy but also to its implementation, frequently is not realized when members have been left out of policy decisions when they could have contributed. Getting the staff, committee, or group to accept responsibility for making decisions, creating conditions that permit effective and wider discussion and participation, and starting and ending a meeting on schedule are factors leading to satisfaction with the use of groups for decision-making purposes.

Authority relations between the leader and group members also occur in staff and other types of meetings. Dependent reactions arise where members want the chairman or leader to "tell the group what to do." Resistance toward leadership occurs when members contest proposals just because they are from the leader.

Member Reactions and Behavior

A typical negative reaction toward the leader is expressed by subordinates in the remark, "While it is *our* responsibility to compose the agenda, the leader actually controls what gets discussed." Other criticisms are, "He goes around the group pinpointing us for our individual reactions. He puts us on the spot"; or "He pushes us to a decision before we are ready." Too many meetings needed to get decisions, emotional reactions to favoritism, and poor procedures for appointing subcommittees are regarded as evidences of poor leadership.

The commonness of group and staff meetings throughout industrial situations, the unsatisfactory manner with which they frequently are conducted, and their recognized importance for policy decisions justify the heavy emphasis in human relations of training for making meetings more effective.

Human Relations Problems Related to Organization within Departments

Difficulties at the departmental level are prominent. The department is a formal control unit with the characteristics of an enduring organization. Within it there are explicit group and individual standards for work and other types of conduct, fixed communication channels, and factors that determine morale. Also included is the informal level based on personal acceptances and rejections.

Frequently recognized are problems arising from incompatability of department personnel where the friction seems to be based on conflicting personalities. Use of a combination of group therapy with roleplaying to investigate such problems is described by Speroff (79). There is evidence that preferred treatment of departmental personnel by superiors produces competition, jealousy, rivalry, and conflict. The conflict produced is not determined solely by personality, but also by situational factors. Another problem is in situations where there are two or more "strong" or influential persons competing with one another and forcing other members to align themselves into subgroups or cliques. The result is divided loyalties and internal discord. Roleplaying approaches to loyalty problems are reported by Symonds (94). Roleplaying to increase acquaintance with problems of people in other positions is cited by Speroff (80).

The need in many departments is to create flexibility so that members help one another rather than simply doing their own jobs. This is in part a morale or *esprit de corps* problem. Informal standards and interpersonal relationships through which members can "take the roles of one another," and accept shared responsibility for total output as well as personal responsibility for individual work are lacking. Creating conditions where members see and feel that over-all responsibility to the department is as important as personal work is a basic problem.

Introducing changes in customary patterns of work is a source of conflict at departmental and divisional levels. Changes proposed by superiors are likely to be viewed with suspicion and distrust by subordinates. A remark, "I knew it would fail, but no one sought my advice about it; I'm glad it did," is typical. When a person feels that he should have been consulted but was not, either he has misunderstood his role or his superiors failed to recognize his potential contribu-

42

tions. Another type of difficulty may occur when a person is called on to introduce changes in his department but he creates the impression that the department is "free" to influence the proposed changes. The superior then is the victim of conflicting pressures. On one side he is obligated to make the designated change. On the other, he has committed himself to his subordinates to introduce a different change. Resentment, withdrawal, or hostility toward the superior result from this type of dilemma. Introducing changes in work patterns is basic to effective department functioning. The *way* a change is brought about is important from a human relations point of view, and is a source of problems to those responsible for the management of departments. Haire has discussed the use of roleplaying to investigate group situations of the kind discussed (36).

Interdepartmental and Intergroup Relations

Relationships between departments are another source of interpersonal difficulties. Some disturbances arise in connection with poor communication. They may be due to the absence of formal channels for transmitting information from one department to another. Inappropriate and uncontrolled informal channels may carry rumor, scuttlebutt, and innuendo. Other problems occur when representatives of departments don't share information with one another. Loyalty to one's own department prevents giving unfavorable in-group information to the representative of another department. From another point of view, reporting unfavorable in-group information to someone from another department can be a way of expressing hostility toward one's own work group. In both cases distorted information may produce conflict both between departments and between members within a department.

The department is a group which rewards and punishes its members. In-group feelings are likely to develop and to be the basis for competitive feelings toward "outside" groups. A need may be present to withhold information so that the internal strength of one's own group can be maintained. Loyalty to one's own group at the expense of other groups is likely to decrease the effectiveness of the total organization. Frictions between management and labor indicate the tremendous range of problems between groups within an organization. Roleplay applications in this area are provided by Liveright (45), Lonergan (47), Fantel (28), and Speroff (82).

Organizational Design

The over-all format of an organization is based on a number of assumptions about human factors which may be the source of many difficulties. Where decisions are made, how lower levels of an organization are controlled, number of positions from the bottom to the top of the organization, span of control concepts, and so on, are factors which often create conditions of hostility and friction which may be resolved only through alterations in the organization itself. Additional problems arise between an organization and the community, the public that it serves, and its stockholders. A striking example of roleplaying used to evaluate a total organization is presented in the 1956 *Proceedings* of the Human Relations Training Laboratory.[2]

Summary

This survey of human problems in work permits one to focus the issue. The question is, "How can such problems be

2. *Proceedings.* The Human Relations Training Laboratory. Las Vegas, New Mexico: 1956.

approached so that there is a possibility of solving them?" Must problems of the kind that have been given as examples persist simply because they have always been with us, or is there a possibility of finding answers and solutions for them? There are three good answers: better *training,* better *evaluation,* and better *instruction.* Roleplaying methods are suitable for helping individuals and groups to develop sensitivity and skill in analyzing situations and in dealing with people-type problems.

Is roleplaying acceptable at managerial levels? Shaw has investigated this question and reports that 79 per cent of a sample of participants in an American Management Association course accepted this method of training (76). A comparable figure of 78 per cent was obtained by Lonergan with management trainees (48).

The evidence at hand therefore leads us to two conclusions. Common and persistent human relations problems in business and industry can be effectively handled by roleplaying methods. Evidence for this comes through theory and through experience. Also, such procedures are acceptable by people on both sides of the organizational table, and have been found satisfactory in use.

The problem for those in organizations who wish to try these new procedures is how to use them. This practical problem is the concern of the rest of this book.

TECHNIQUES

Preparations

ROLEPLAYING MAY TAKE PLACE under a variety of circumstances, in almost any locale, and with almost any individual or group. The successful use of the procedure depends on many factors, among which are proper preparations, which in turn depend crucially on understanding the structure of the group, the dynamics of the milieu and the aims of individual participants. The kinds of problems taken up, and the kind of roleplaying done depend for satisfaction on a comprehensive knowledge of the entire situation. Even with this understanding, the roleplaying director must still arrange conditions to ensure a reasonable degree of success. It is not enough for a director to enter any situation at any time without knowledge of what is going on and begin roleplaying. The psychological milieu, the individuals, and the circumstances must be prepared, and the director should have a fairly clear notion of what he should do.

Roleplaying is a spontaneity technique. The director can arrange situations so that the individuals participating will say and do things they ordinarily might not in ordinary life, but the consequences of their roleplaying behavior may not

48

be in the desired direction, if the director works in the dark. Proper preparation is essential, otherwise roleplaying may fall flat.

To cite an example: in the first session of an indigenous group, a director who did not know that the members were in fierce competition with one another, and that the entire group was in a chronic state of anxiety, decided to demonstrate the potentialities of roleplaying to prove that the procedure was not a "game of playacting" but that it could elicit powerful emotions. A volunteer was asked to play the role of a supervisor to show how he would handle a problem of two bickering employees. He was motivated to do his best by being told in front of the group that he would be rated for the speed and the quality of his capacity to adjudicate a dispute. He sat behind a desk in front of some twenty of his colleagues and prepared to show what he could do.

The director then selected two additional members, asking them to play the part of employees with a problem, who were to go to the "supervisor" to have him settle the dispute. Privately, he whispered to them that they were not to let the protagonist know exactly what the problem was, but to show great excitement and anger. The purpose was, the director told the two antagonists, to show how the "supervisor" would react to an impossible situation.

When the antagonists showed up, they simulated anger calling each other names and they demanded from their supervisor an immediate solution to their conflict. The "director" tried to find out what was bothering them but was not able to get this information, for one antagonist would respond: "*You* know what it is. It is the same old problem." The other would reply: "Yes. And I want an immediate answer." To which the other antagonist would answer: "I told you a million times, and you told him so yourself, so now you should settle this once and for all." The supervisor who was trying to calm the individuals and learn what the problem was became frustrated and upset, and so made a sad spectacle of himself.

At this point the director stopped the session and explained to the group that he had demonstrated what he was interested in. He tried to point out the protagonist had been put in an impossible situation—but to no avail. Not only was the protagonist upset but the entire group was so shaken up by the experience that every individual refused to have anything further to do with roleplaying.

From this example one can see that using roleplaying effectively depends on many variables. The good sense of the director is most important. The intelligent director prepares himself, the participants, and the individuals in the psychological milieu as well as in the environmental space to ensure success.

Let us first consider how "outsiders" should be prepared—individuals who are part of the general milieu in which the roleplayers interact. We may consider these individuals in terms of three layers: executives, middle management, and hourly employees.

Executive Level

Generally speaking, the roleplaying director will find that executives who are not to participate directly in roleplaying, will take a sympathetic attitude to intensive training. It is generally best for the roleplaying director to meet with key executives, either in individual interviews or in a group meeting, to give them a frank exposition of the nature and values of roleplaying, pointing out its limitations and dangers. The roleplaying director should explain that he can operate at various levels of sensitivity and that he can control the degree and intensity of the interactions depending on the tolerance shown by the executives. He should state that since roleplaying is a spontaneity situation, people may say and do things they might not otherwise. He should indicate that frequently in even the best organizations, there exist considerable covert tensions. If people with unstable personalities are in a group unexpected reactions may occur.

He should point out that ordinarily people can and will control themselves, and that roleplaying is directed ordinarily to nonsensitive issues at least in the early stages, but since almost anything can happen during the heat of acting out, he would like to be certain of the degree of tolerance that the executives can take.

He may give examples, such as the following: In a university-sponsored roleplaying group, a protagonist interacting with his "president" made a number of highly aggressive and disparaging remarks in the most unflattering manner. Later, this individual told the director that he had gone farther than he had wanted, and was certain that if information reached the president about what he had said that he would be out of a job.

The director may point out that the very things that make roleplaying valuable are those that might make it dangerous— its potentialities to get people to release themselves and speak out their thoughts, but that this ventilation with subsequent discussions might well be of the utmost value.

Middle Levels

Most industrial roleplaying is directed to individuals at the middle level of management—employees below the policy making level and above the level of hourly employees. Such individuals are on their way up, and tend to be extremely competitive. There is always the problem of extreme sensitivity in dealing with these people who tend to be quite suspicious of procedures which may affect their relative status in an organization. Consequently, they must be handled with great tact and sensitivity.

In "selling" roleplaying to them, emphasis should be placed on technical rather than personal values. Despite the fact that necessary improvements often depend on traits such as insight, empathy, self-assurance, control, etc., the director should emphasize nonsensitive potentialities such as skills and information. To do this, probably the best way to proceed is to discuss roleplaying with small groups of individuals in a more-or-less relaxed atmosphere. In this manner the director can not only reduce the anxieties of the individuals but can also obtain valuable insights about individual and group problems.

Hourly Levels

Roleplaying is rarely offered to people at the hourly level of employment, and therefore the problem of selling roleplaying to this group does not frequently occur. The manner of dealing with hourly employees is the same as dealing with middle management groups. They should be given information about roleplaying, since they may find out that they were discussed. An employee who finds out that his supervisor talked about him in a group and that someone acted his part may become upset.

Probably the best way of handling this type of situation is to ask participants to clear any acting with the people involved—to get permission to take up any particular situation—which in itself can frequently do a great deal toward improvement of any problem.

At this point we may refer to the issue of "leaks." Ordinarily in training groups, members respect the privacy of the group, and they tend to keep any information they obtain to themselves. In early sessions usually very little sensitive material comes out, and touchy situations tend to emerge only much later when every member feels comfortable at which time the group tends to form a protective iron curtain about itself.

Summarizing some of these ideas, the wise director will try to communicate to others what roleplaying is and what it can do, and will try to learn as much as possible about the nature of the milieu so that he can operate in as intelligent a manner as possible. In the meantime he tends to create within the group a climate of relative freedom and acceptance so that if an equivocal situation arises a favorable attitude toward him and his work will exist.

We have above perhaps taken an unduly conservative position, pointing out the dangers, but since in real life dangers do occur, it is important to know how they can be reduced through clear communication.

The Environment

Successful roleplaying depends on the physical location and surroundings in which it takes place. The wise director tries to obtain an optimal location for his work, and he tries to arrange convenient schedules.

Location

The ideal location has these characteristics:

Proper Size. The room should have a minimum of 25 to a maximum of 50 square feet per participant. Very small or very large rooms are not suitable. If one has to make a choice between two unsuitable locations, a smaller room is generally preferred.

Privacy. The roleplaying location should have no distractions. No one should enter the room or be able to look into it while a session is going on. Participants should not be interrupted by telephone calls or visitors. The room should be quiet, and extraneous noises such as peoples' voices should be kept out.

Flexibility. The room should not have fixed furniture. A class room with bolted seats or an auditorium are examples of poor locations.

It is frequently difficult to obtain a proper location, but the ingenious director may be able to requisition a room, such as an executive office, to meet his needs. He should feel that nothing is too good for his purposes.

Scheduling

To arrange a schedule not unduly irksome to all involved may be a difficult problem. A schedule convenient for individuals may be inconvenient for the company. The director should be aware that compromises have to be made. But unless the time selected is such to permit him to do his work adequately, he should properly refuse to carry on.

The main point made in the above section is that the director should make proper preparations about time and place to permit him to work to an optimal degree of success.

Arrangements

Now that we have discussed place and scheduling, the next issue refers to the arrangements, that is to say, the placement of the furniture and the requisition of materials. With respect to furniture, the general rule is that there should be no excess pieces in the room beyond those needed, and that items should be so arranged as to permit maximal visual and auditory communication between all members. A long conference room with a narrow table is an example of a particularly poor arrangement.

Extra pieces of furniture should be removed from the room if possible; if not, they should be grouped in a corner out of the way, and if possible separated from the rest of the room by screens. Chairs and tables to be used should be neatly arranged so the individuals will go to their proper places without any difficulty.

Personnel

Roleplaying is a technique like the interview, and with a little instruction any person capable of carrying an effective interview can learn to conduct roleplaying. Roleplaying directors come in all sizes and shapes as it were, and are probably no more alike in their personalities, abilities, or backgrounds than training directors. However, we can make some generalizations about the important qualifications, personal and technical of good directors.

Personal Qualifications

The good director should be an "open" rather than a "closed" type of person. That is to say he should be friendly and flexible. He has a good sense of orientation, which means he can see the trees *and* the forest in any problem. He knows what is going on, and has a keen sense of awareness of the relative importance of situations. He must have adroitness, or the tact and sensitivity to deal with people and the capacity to straighten out complexities and entanglements. He is persuasive, and can get people to understand what is going on and to want to participate. He has good judgment and can assess situations and make rapid decisions of good quality. He must, perhaps above all, have assurance that what he is doing is worth-while and that he can handle the situation.

55

This will show itself in his courage and tolerance, and his capacity to avoid becoming flustered or uncertain. Beyond all these qualities, the really good director has sincerity. He is interested in people and sincerely wants to be of help to them.

This combination of qualities will give individuals confidence in the director, and will facilitate the movement desired. The "personality" of the director is of far greater importance than his technical qualifications, which we shall discuss below.

Training

At the present time we have no reliable information regarding the necessary background training that a roleplaying director should have. There is no reason to believe that a director trained in the social sciences is any better than one trained in the biological or physical sciences; that a psychologist is any better than a teacher; or a teacher any better than an engineer. It is not known whether a college graduate is necessarily any better than one who has not finished high school. However, it would appear, everything else being constant, that the best prepared individuals are those people who have a good background in the behavioral sciences, trained in human relations areas. However, some academically poorly prepared individuals are sometimes found to be "naturals" for roleplaying and superior to people with excellent academic backgrounds.

If it is kept in mind that roleplaying may have many levels of competence, and that for some levels high degrees of ability are not necessary, even poorly trained and poorly qualified people can do satisfactory jobs when not too much skill is called for. No matter how poorly prepared a director may be, he can improve his understanding and capacity by proper preparation—through reading and study, but most of all by observation and participation in other roleplaying groups. The conscientious director will take advantage of courses and seminars given in this area by universities and private consulting firms, as well as by professional societies. In the appendix we list some organizations that provide roleplaying training.

Functions

The roleplaying director need not be an expert in the field of specialization of the group participants. He is a facilitator, not a teacher. One of the writers of this book has done roleplaying with teachers, nurses, prison guards, army officers, salesmen, business executives and training directors.

If the director should happen to have technical knowledge of the field in which the participants are interested, he may suppress this information, if he does not wish to confuse his role as a facilitator with that of instructor. But if he is a specialist in the particular area, he may wish to become a resource person who may then inject his opinions with reference to proper role behavior. But it is usually wise for him not to try to play the role of the director and the expert.

Assistants

In most cases the director works alone. However, he may have assistants. These individuals do not attend sessions primarily for their own benefit, but rather to assist the director in his work. They serve two general roles: as antagonists and as observers.

Antagonists. The primary person in a roleplaying session is called a protagonist. He is the one who is to be trained or evaluated. He interacts with other individuals who may take a variety of roles, called antagonists, even though there may not necessarily be any conflict in the role situation. These antagonists generally come from the group: sometimes being selected by the protagonist himself, sometimes being volunteers and sometimes being assigned by the director.

57

A trained assistant who serves as an antagonist is frequently useful, especially when roleplaying is done for information-giving or for testing. The trained assistant operates in a more uniform manner than would one who is not trained, and he provides a more constant stimulus to the protagonist. Trained assistants are especially valuable in the "doubling" and the "private thoughts" techniques, (page 85) becoming sensitized to how people think. In using complicated techniques, or when multiple groups are employed, such assistants can be invaluable in reducing confusion.

Observers. Frequently, the director wishes to have assistants serve as nonparticipating observers, reporting back to the group their observations and conclusions. While some members of any group can be impressed into these roles, trained observers, especially those who have observed similar situations in other groups can be extremely helpful. Not being personally involved with the training situation nor with the individuals, these assistants provide expert objective summaries and evaluations. If somewhat complicated observer guides are used with a group that will not meet enough times to make these forms understood, the assistants can employ them economically. When a group of trained observers have a general understanding of the director's purposes, they can function to assist the group in its development.

Materials

Depending on the purposes of roleplaying, certain materials may be helpful. For a group that will continue for a long time and which is primarily interested in personality improvement, relatively little material is required. The group meets in a circle and the space in the center becomes the "roleplaying stage." However, in other groups, especially large ones, a platform should be provided, and one about one foot in height and about eight by eight feet in dimensions is sufficient. In addition, a blackboard or a chart pad may be helpful. A recording device such as a tape recorder is frequently very useful. A dummy telephone and a timer may also at times be valuable.

In some cases the director will hand out case material to the participants of the kind found in the appendix. Usually when large groups are involved, it is best to arrange the various instructions into packets, either clipped together or stapled. In some cases it may be advantageous for the various roles to be duplicated on different colored paper, so that the participant who plays the role of the "supervisor" will read his instructions from a white sheet, the "salesman" from a yellow sheet, etc.

When guides are employed, especially of the kind that call for multiple observations and recordings, participants should be given looseleaf note books in which they can conveniently keep records of their development.

Summary

Perfection depends on trifles, but that perfection is not a trifle is a trite but true remark. Successful roleplaying depends on many interlocking and interacting elements, and crucially calls for adequate preparation. One element that is out of kilter, such as a too-short extension cord for the tape recorder, or a microphone that does not work, or the loss of case material, or misunderstandings by one or more members may throw a session out of functional commission. The wise director plans his sessions well, and his art depends to a great extent on appearing to be natural, easy and spontaneous, which frequently calls for considerable prior work. What he does in a session represents only a small fraction of what he does over-all.

Directing Roleplaying

A NUMBER OF PEOPLE have identified various phases in roleplaying. Shaw (75) suggests three parts: (a) warm up, (b) enactment, and (c) postsession analysis. In an anonymously written article (2) five phases are suggested: (a) establish principles, (b) brief on problems, (c) act out, (d) make recordings, and (e) have discussions. Liveright (45) lists six divisions: (a) choose problem, (b) agree on details, (c) define roles, (d) instruct observers, (e) act out, and (f) discuss. Bavelas (10) suggests no fewer than 14 steps which the reader will find summarized in the annotated bibliography on page 220.

In this chapter we shall use a four-step sequence of phases:

A. *Plan*—Determining purposes and procedures for individual sessions and for an entire sequence of sessions.

B. *Acclimate*—Developing a proper climate for the group and warming up the group for individual sessions.

C. *Enact*—Proceeding with the sessions proper in conducting roleplaying.

D. *Feedback*—Conducting discussions and analyzing roleplaying.

60

Planning

The amount of planning may vary considerably for any session or sequence of sessions. If the roleplaying is for testing or informing, considerable pre-planning is usually required. If the sessions are for training, a lesser amount of planning is usually needed. For unstructured training situations, relatively little planning is called for.

Organizations

Ordinarily, the desires of enterprises supporting roleplaying are clear enough. The director should take pains to determine as explicitly as possible what the executives in the organization really want from roleplaying. A clarification helps the executives and the director to arrive at a common understanding of goals to be achieved, and leads to satisfaction on both sides.

A problem occurs when people come for training from a number of enterprises. In some cases, skill development may be the major issue; in other cases, personality readjustment is desired. While such aims are not mutually incompatible, it is preferable that members in any group have more-or-less uniform desires. For this reason, should there be incompatible demands, it is best on finding out what they are to readjust schedules or groups to form as homogeneous a group as possible in terms of intentions.

Individuals

The director should know what the trainees want from roleplaying training. A simple way is to begin a session with a group discussion of individual aims. Another way is individual or small group interviews. Another procedure is questionnaires. In any event, the director should have a fairly clear understanding of the problems and the expectations of group members. Knowing this, he can modify and control roleplaying to attain relative satisfaction. There is little point in the director proceeding on the basis of hypotheses he may have about wants which may be counter to the desires of the group members. Success in roleplaying, especially when used for training, depends on mutual alignment of goals. As sessions continue, the director begins to know the individuals and begins to understand their weaknesses. He can now begin to design situations intended to meet specific problems. This can best be done co-operatively: either by calling members for interviews or else by involving the entire group in discussions to this end. By use of universal observation sheets such as those shown on page 211 this diagnostic process can be facilitated.

Climate

In every group and at any time individual members have particular attitudes to the group process. There are many ways of illustrating attitudes, but a triangular map, the corners of which are labeled "Fight—Flight—Work" seems satisfactory. Any individual can be placed somewhere on this map, and a central point may be used to indicate the consensus of the group. Those individuals who fit in the *fight* corner are actively hostile, and are attending because they are forced to do so. Those in the *flight* corner are resistant, and do not want to participate. Those in the *work* corner, on the other hand, are highly motivated to participate. Figure 1 indicates how a typical beginning group may look.

The major immediate purpose of the director is to "warm up" the group so that every member will move closer to the *work* position as illustrated in Figure 2.

62

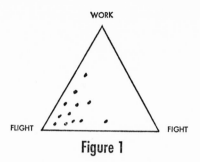

Figure 1

To give an example of how this map may be used, an incident may be recounted. The president of a company decided that certain people in his organization should enroll in a training course. He interviewed the individuals he felt would benefit,

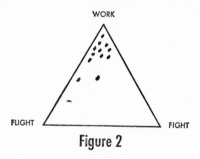

Figure 2

each of whom accepted training. The sessions were to take place on a Saturday. The training director sensed the unfavorable attitude of the group and so he asked each member to draw a triangle on a small piece of paper and to place a dot to indicate his attitude to the session. The president was then asked to estimate the average position of the dots. When, on a blackboard his prediction—"work"—was contrasted with the actual individual placements, a considerable discrepancy was seen for the majority of the members' dots were along the lower left corner near "flight"!

Whatever may be the original attitudes of the members, it is

63

the responsibility of the director to improve them if they are not ideal. In some cases this is difficult. People forced to attend will usually feel antagonistic. If the group consists of people who know one another, and who feel the sessions may affect their prestige, this is another difficult situation. If people in hierarchical relations to each other are in a group, relationships are frequently difficult to adjust. One very powerful and influential person in a group can affect the necessary attitude of *work* required for good roleplaying. An individual who is not trusted by others may also affect a group. The experienced director will try to assay the situation, either by interview, group discussions, or sociometric analyses — and depending on the strengths of attitudes will, if possible, make modifications in the group composition before beginning. Below is an illustration of a simple sociometric procedure which permits the director to understand the relationships of people to each other in an indigenous group.

Every member is asked to write down three names on a piece of paper of people with whom the individual would like to work in a subgroup. Assuming for the purpose of illustration, a group of eight people, let us say that the following results are obtained upon tabulation.

Sociometric Summary of a Group

Name of Participant	Number who want to be paired with him
Abt	5
Bay	—
Cor	3
Dee	3
Ego	4
Fee	3
Gon	2
Ham	4

On the basis of a system as simple as this, it becomes evident that Bay is undesirable in this group since no one wants to work with him. Knowing this permits the director to make suitable modifications in the composition of the group, or at least deal with the problem more effectively.

Feelings about the group as a whole and about the members are not too important when the roleplaying is given for testing or demonstration; or when there is to be only one training session. When a group is to meet over a considerable period of time for many sessions this is another matter: then the director is wise to do something immediately to change the composition of a group with incompatible members to ensure some degree of success in his operations. While this is not a frequent problem, it would be particularly distressing were an ill-mated group to be assembled without the director having any awareness of the fact—and then for him to attribute the failure of the group either to himself or the procedure.

Changing the Climate

The director has the responsibility of getting people to want to work. Understanding that attitudes can be changed, he must have some strategy in mind. Below we shall discuss some techniques that may be used to change attitudes from *flight* or *fight* to *work*.

Gradualism. It is stated that a frog can be boiled to death without his apparently realizing it, if the water's temperature can be raised very gradually. Regardless of the truth of this, a good procedure in starting roleplaying is to operate in so gradual a manner that people are subtly introduced to it so they become involved in the process without suffering a transitional period. Below are some specific techniques in illustration.

The director may begin with lectures and discussions on problems, and then may roleplay a problem himself with an assistant, or may ask some assistants to roleplay a related problem for illustrative purposes. In this way the members get to know what roleplaying is, they will discuss performances, and get used to the idea of the procedure.

A second method may be to interview some members privately and ask them to play certain roles at the next session. The director may take the role of the antagonist with them privately for rehearsal purposes, which may be called roleplaying for roleplaying!

Another variation calls for a demonstration by the director and an assistant, assistants alone, or members who have been prepared, and then asking the group to break up into smaller "buzz" groups to roleplay the parts they have observed.

Discussions. After every phase, the director should non-directively lead a discussion, being careful not to be defensive about the technique. It is not unusual for some people to express very negative attitudes about roleplaying in the beginning and they may try to lead a general rebellion especially among others who feel threatened. By permitting full discussions of the procedure when there is uneasiness about roleplaying, eventually defenders of this procedure will arise, and finally an accepting attitude will emerge. In one case, an individual led an attack after a demonstration. He argued that the real purpose of training was "to learn" and that this method was "artificial and useless." That same session he participated in roleplaying and later made just as strong a positive assertion that roleplaying was "the real thing ... You learn a lot from it."

Enactments

Let us assume that a group's climate is such that members are eager to work. We now come to the question of directing enactments. How this is done will depend on the individual

66

director and the group. Some typical procedures shall be illustrated.

Structuring the Session

The director should have some kind of a timetable for sessions. Let us say that a meeting is to last about 90 minutes, which seems to be about the optimal time for sessions. He may decide that he will have first a general discussion of the particular issue to be taken up at the meeting, then enactment by multiple roleplaying of a problem, and then further analysis and discussion of the issue. If he has some sort of a schedule, he can proceed in an organized manner which will give members a feeling of security based on the knowledge that the director knows what he is doing.

Presenting the Problem. Let us assume that one particular session is to be devoted to the handling of hostility. The director may have prepared a demonstration case. He may begin with a lecture on the question, examples of typical problems, and then lead a discussion. When he feels the group has become motivated and interested he may then proceed to an enactment of the demonstration case.

Obtaining Participants. The director may now state that he has a case problem and would like to have volunteers to demonstrate it. He must be careful not to press anyone to volunteer. It is best at this point to wait patiently for people to emerge from the group. If no one offers to participate after a full 60 seconds of silence, the director may volunteer himself. Usually, however, someone will accept the challenge if the director can wait long enough.

Preparing. If the enactment is to start with printed material, various participants can read their instructions silently and after they understand them, can act them out. There are many variations possible, some of which we shall discuss below.

1. Have two sets of participants read the instructions, and while the first set is acting in front of the group, the second set is kept out of the room, so they do not see the first set role-playing. Immediately upon completion of the first enactment, the second set of roleplayers come in to re-play the same problem. This permits the group to see how different individuals handle the same problem. Another variation is to use the same antagonist against two protagonists, each of whom has independently prepared for the situation.

2. Have several sets of participants. All those who are to take a particular role can discuss proper ways of handling the problem. If the roles are about Abt and his antagonist Bay, all the Abts can discuss how Abt should handle his problem, and at the same time the Bays meet for the same reason. After the Abts and the Bays have discussed their roles, one Abt and one Bay act out the problem in front of the group. Then, either new enactments by another set of Abts and Bays can occur, or else a general analysis may take place.

3. Read the roles to the entire group. The group then discusses how the problem should be handled. Volunteers are obtained and the problem is enacted. After enactment, further discussions may ensue, resulting in new suggestions for proper handling, and then there can be another enactment also followed by discussions.

Instead of being limited by reading a problem and simple enactment, the director may introduce variations. It is in the subtleties of these variations that a director begins to deal with specific individual and group needs. The procedure discussed below is an example of flexible roleplaying.

Let us assume that the roleplaying director is working with a group of foremen and they have a common problem as follows: they supervise workers who run semiautomatic machines. The workers frequently leave machines for coffee-breaks, socializations, etc. The machines run themselves, but should something go wrong, then a great deal of wastage and even damage to very expensive machines may occur. However, many workers take chances and leave the machines unattended, sometimes for as long as an hour. Once in a very long time something does go wrong. If the operator is on the spot, he can stop the machine immediately, thus minimizing the damage. If he is away, many thousands of dollars of wastage or damage may occur. The foremen in the group are plagued by this common problem, and the director decides to try to build up a roleplaying situation to help them learn how to deal with it.

The director's name is Yew, and the group members' names are Abt, Bay, Cor, Dee, Ego, and Fee.

YEW: For this problem, can we get someone to take the role of the foreman? I suppose each of you has had experience with this matter.

FEE: I'll take it.

YEW: How do you see your role as foreman?

FEE: Well, it's just the way we said. The men have got to stay by their machines. It's true there's rarely anything wrong, but when there is, we want the men there.

YEW: Why don't they stay?

FEE: Well, they have a million excuses.

YEW: Let's see what it looks like in action. Fee will act as the foreman, the rest of you will represent his crew. But I think we should have Fee's supervisor, too. Who could take that role?

ABT: I could.

YEW: Abt, have you ever had your own supervisor discuss this problem with you?

ABT: Many times.

YEW: Let us now try two roleplaying situations. The first one will be between Abt, the supervisor, and Fee the foreman. Abt, you will tell Fee what you want him to do in reference to the problem of people leaving their machines unattended. Then Fee, you call a meeting of your men and you tell them what the situation is and what you want them to do. Is everything clear to everyone? Fine, let us go ahead.

❊ ❊ ❊

ABT: Say Fee, I want to talk to you.

FEE: Yes, Mr. Abt.

ABT: Now Fee, you're the foreman and you're responsible for your men. You know and I know that they are exceeding the limits of what's right. I want to see the men where they belong. Only last night I found four of them having coffee, and you know that's not right. Suppose one of the machines started acting up? By the time they'd get to the machine, more than a year's salary might be gone up in smoke. Every second counts in an emergency. Those machines can't think for themselves. Now, you've come up from the ranks and you were a good worker, and I don't want to see you get in trouble—and I don't want to get in trouble. So, it's up to you to do what's right. I don't want to discuss this with you again.

FEE: Yes Sir, I'll talk to the men.

❊ ❊ ❊

YEW: Fine, let's stop there. We now have the background of the problem. Abt, the supervisor, has told Fee what he has to do. Now, Fee is going to call a meeting with his men. Each of you try to act the part of some of the people you actually supervise, taking up all the arguments they give. We shall watch how Mr. Fee handles the problem. Let us say it is now the end of the work day and Mr. Fee calls you into his office for a short talk. Let's see how Fee would do it. Ready?

❊ ❊ ❊

FEE: Fellows, I have to take up something with you and I'm dead serious.

COR: What is it Mr. Fee?

FEE: This morning Mr. Abt talked to me. It's my neck he was talking about. I want to get along with you guys, but you are really going too far. I want you on the machines, and that's all there is to it.

COR: We know that.

FEE: He caught you having coffee last night.

COR: Not me.

FEE: I don't know who it was, but I'm warning each and every one of you to watch those machines.

70

DEE: Now just a minute, can't we even go to the toilet or nothing?

EGO: I've been on the job six years and nothing has ever happened. You can go crazy just watching and waiting. I know my machine. When there's anything wrong with it, I stay with it. When it's humming along, maybe I go away for a couple of minutes, but nothing has ever happened.

DEE: Why are you taking it out on us? Abt doesn't know what it's all about.

FEE: Maybe he doesn't but he's my boss, and what he says goes. Either you guys stick to your machines or else...

BAY: Or else what?

FEE: You know what else!

DEE: I don't think your attitude is right. Everybody knows that we are careful. I never leave my machine unless it's going OK and unless someone is covering me. I don't think it's fair for you to just get mad because Abt is bothering you.

FEE: Well, you know my instructions and orders. You just keep to your machines.

YEW: (Clapping hands.) OK, let's stop and discuss what happened...

Leading the Group

The roleplaying director has a rather difficult role to play in the group. He should follow a line of nonauthority with reference to the *content* of sessions but should be the authority with reference to the *functions* of the group. The closest example might be the position of a judge in a court, who starts sessions, keeps procedures moving, settles procedural issues, but does not interject his own opinions about the merits of the case. He is the arbiter of functions, but not of issues.

Some tips may be of value with reference to running sessions:

1. Try to have a timetable.

2. Have the strategy of sessions well worked out in your mind, keeping in mind the three phases of *warm up, enactment* and *feedback*.

71

3. Talk as little as possible. You are not serving as an authority on the problem, so keep your opinions to yourself. Avoid lecturing.

4. Try to get the group to accept your authority in conducting sessions.

5. Set aside time regularly for analysis of your leadership. This "feedback" is important for your own development and improved handling of situations.

Creative Roleplaying

When the director has a prior idea or information about the problem to be acted, he can plan in advance how to conduct the session. To direct cases when one has scripts as outlines is not too difficult. A more difficult situation occurs when the director begins with literally nothing, and looks for material from the individuals in the group. We may call this "creative roleplaying." Now the group and the director have to be flexible, and they act out material from whatever arises from the group. This "free" or "unstructured" type of approach resembles roleplaying procedures in group psychotherapy (29). Its success depends on the director's ability to utilize meaningfully personal problems, and to devise siuations designed to help an individual learn his difficulties and practice ways of improvement.

Below are some general rules for creative roleplaying. However, in this form, rules are made to be broken, since the director becomes more of a professional helper rather than a technical director.

1. Let the protagonist talk himself out. The director should, by questioning, get the individual to give as much explanation as possible about his problem.

2. Obtain as much group involvement in the discussions as

possible, avoiding giving solutions, advice, and other "helpful" suggestions.

3. Try to focus on examples of the problem in action. Use the "W" suggestions—When? Where? Why? What? Who?—to obtain a clear picture of the problem, and then set up one or more situations.

4. Let the protagonist select his own antagonists, and then let him fill in their personality and position. Let each antagonist question the protagonist so that he will be sure he understands his relation to the problem.

5. The director now structures the situation, and gives various members direction. He may ask particular members to stress various elements of the situation to be enacted.

6. The protagonist is asked to stop the action any time he wishes—to inform antagonists how they should play their parts if they are not in keeping with reality, or to point out any particular difficulty which he is having in the production, or generally in life.

7. The director stops the situation whenever he feels enough material has been obtained to permit discussion. Ten minutes is a safe maximum.

8. Discussion of the situation may take place immediately, or may be referred to a later session.

9. After analysis and discussion, the same or a similar situation may again be re-enacted, and further analysis and discussion takes place.

As can be seen, this is the most personal use of roleplaying, and calls not only for a great amount of skill on the part of the director, but also a climate of complete acceptance on the part of group members. Ordinarily, creative roleplaying does not occur until the director and members have established a rather close relationship; coming to a point where they can trust one another. Considerable emotionalism and tension may be generated in creative roleplaying situations.

Feedback

Effective learning depends on feedback. In order to improve, an individual must have information about his progress. Let us take some common examples. If a person is practicing standing on his head, he is instantly aware of whether or not he is doing things right; if he should make any mistake he learns immediately because gravity "feeds back" necessary information about what he is doing, right or wrong. In learning a poem by heart, the individual recites it and soon realizes whether he can go through it without error. In learning to spell, it is common for the learner to ask someone to listen and inform him whether he is catching on. In learning how to swim, the person soon learns that some behavior is unsatisfactory, and that other behavior leads to success. In academic classes, examinations give the student information as to how he is doing and in which areas he is weak. Learning means adopting different or new habit patterns. To know whether we are learning, or have learned, there must be some kind of test. In some cases, as in the head-standing example, or in swimming, or in making sales, or in dealing with people in particular situations, one can "feed back" information to himself without any need for outside confirmations. In other cases, such as learning how to sing, or how to do fine manual work, outside evaluations can be of help.

It must seem very peculiar that people will learn unsuccessful, complex life procedures, and seem to be unable to change them. Some of this can be explained as due to insufficient or unsatisfactory feedback; or even to rejection of feed-

74

back information. Before discussing how feedback is used in roleplaying, let us consider some theoretical aspects of this phenomenon.

Theory

Incredible as it may seem, people rarely really understand themselves. Evidence comes from a variety of areas. For example, it is well known that people do not hear themselves. It is common for an individual on hearing his voice over a tape recorder to be astounded at how he sounds to others. The whole purpose of psychotherapy may be considered to be the attainment of insight or understanding of one's self. It is very common for individuals to arrive at evaluations of their behavior after psychotherapy, quite different from those previously held.

People characterized by others as "selfish," "aggressive," "abrupt," "domineering," etc., ordinarily would deny the truth of those statements. They tend to have much more charitable opinions of themselves. The "selfish" person says he is only looking out for his interests and that charity begins at home; the "aggressive" person merely says he is defending himself; and so on. The process of rationalization is carried into all elements of living.

Research on people's opinions of others and of the self indicates that most people have a better opinion of themselves than do others. When individuals fail, they are very likely to blame their failure on others, and have no realization of their own shortcomings.

What contributes to this peculiar state of affairs? There are a number of explanations. First is the unwillingness of others in our environment to tell us unpleasant things. People would rather remain silent than criticize. They know that if they criticize another, that person may be hurt. A second reason for not learning about oneself is due to emotional blocks. We may hear criticism but cannot accept it. We may even attack individuals who say unpleasant things about us, feeling that they have special reasons for making critical remarks. A third reason for not knowing our defects is due to overcompensation. A good many people handle their defects so that strong points are emphasized to the end that weak ones are minimized. Thus a person who is shy may become persistent; an aggressive person takes on a sense of humor, etc.

In life we develop a series of defenses so that we will not be vulnerable to criticism; also we develop a series of compensating mechanisms to undo or minimize the effect of faults. In psychotherapy, an environmental condition of acceptance and safety must be developed which permits patients to explore sensitive feelings and ideas. Much the same should happen in roleplaying for training: the milieu must become such that individuals will be able to criticize and listen to criticism without getting hurt, and so be able to profit. We now can understand the considerable insistence on proper preparation in Chapter IV. When a group has been properly prepared and developed, the individuals, rather than feeling defensive about criticisms, actually welcome them.

Conducting Feedback

There are many ways in which group feedbacking can be done, and in this section we shall discuss some of them. Whether to have group feedbacking, and, if so, which procedure to use and how much time to give it, depends on the judgment of the director. He is aware that successful roleplaying is crucially dependent on effective feedbacking. He must be aware that people are not used to making critical remarks about others, especially to their faces. He realizes that the members will be able to criticize others if he can create the proper climate, and therefore he will operate in such ways as to ensure an attitude of honest criticism.

Free Discussion. The simplest and most common method of directing group feedback is simply to ask the observers and participants to comment on individual performances. Once the group has gotten over its initial hesitation, discussion may be generated. However, it is one thing to have a lot of hot discussion and it is another to have a directed feedback. While in general we would prefer that a director let a group discuss any issue in a free manner, it would be best for him when he notices that the group is wandering to interject remarks calculated to bring them back to the issue at hand. It is very easy for a group to wander off on minor details not pertinent to the central issue of how an individual behaved. Although the director usually does not participate in the discussion, he should take pains to direct comments to pertinent elements.

Buzz Groups. The buzz group is a useful variation of the free discussion. A large group is broken into subgroups with instructions to discuss the performance and to summarize ideas. Various groups may be assigned to specific areas. The consensus of each small group is then reported by a "secretary" to the whole group. The advantage of the buzz groups is that every individual is likely to participate, and since the individual being evaluated is not in every buzz group, a more honest and accurate level of reporting is to be expected. After the secretaries' report the entire group may rediscuss the various issues. While both of these procedures usually take place at the end of a performance, there are times when the action can be broken into, and the director may ask for immediate comments. An illustration may be given below. Fee and Abt may be in the middle of a session, when the following occurs:

FEE: I can only tell you once again, what I have told you already . . .

❖   ❖   ❖

YEW: (Clapping hands twice) Cut! Let's stop and analyze what's going on right this minute. Now, Abt, you're on the stage with Fee. How do you feel about how he's going about it?

ABT: He seems unsure of himself. He doesn't convince me.

YEW: Why?

ABT: I don't know. Just seems that way.

YEW: I interrupted the action at this point to see what opinions any of you may have about Fee at this point. Any comments?

BAY: I noticed he kept fidgeting. His hands went in and out of his pockets, and he kept shuffling from foot to foot. I think he was kind of nervous.

DEE: Also, his voice. He gets kind of shrill when he gets angry.

YEW: What do you think of that, Fee?

FEE: I didn't feel nervous. I always kind of fidget.

YEW: Although you say you don't feel nervous, apparently you give that impression.

ABT: I can answer that. I felt he was tense, and so he made me feel tense, too. I got an uncomfortable feeling about him.

YEW: Well, I wanted to stop the action just for a bit of discussion at this point. Now, can you continue from where I stopped you?

❖   ❖   ❖

FEE: I'll tell you again what I've already told you . . .

Such interruptions can be readily tolerated in training groups. The directors should not hesitate to stop the action when he thinks something worthy of comment has come up, otherwise the situation may get cold for later discussion.

Round Robin. In this procedure each individual is asked to make a short comment, usually a single sentence, with reference to an over-all evaluation of the protagonist. No interruptions are permitted until each member has had his say. While comments are being made, the director, or an assistant, may note the comments, which may be listed on a blackboard, and which later may serve as the basis for group discussions.

The round robin technique has some advantages: it enables each individual to make a comment; because people do not like to repeat what others have said, it forces out new ideas; and it enables a wide variety of comments to be obtained prior to discussion. The classification of comments provides a more-or-less systematic method for analyzing and evaluating specific elements in the protagonist's performance.

Questionnaires. Observers may be given questionnaires with reference to a specific problem. These forms direct the observers to certain facets of behavior, and provide a systematic procedure for evaluation.

Observation Guides. The director may use observation guides. The guides described in the appendix represent a system that can be used not only for discussion purposes but also to record the quality of performance over a number of sessions, so that the development of individuals can be charted. In this manner, areas of strengths and weaknesses can be determined, which in turn, permit the individual participants and the director to know what to emphasize in training situations.

Phonographic Recordings. The tape recorder is a most useful tool for analyzing roleplaying. If the machine has an odometer, a register which indicates specifically where certain phases in the interaction occurred, this is of great advantage. During the enactment, the director or an assistant may make notes indicating at which point on the tape certain events occurred.

After a scene has been played out, the director may then replay the recording, asking members to inform him when to stop the recording for discussion. In this manner, specific elements can be relistened to, and evaluated. In some cases, extended discussions may occur about apparently minor elements, which might be missed during the actual enactment. The director may then have the protagonist replay the situation with the antagonists either in the very same manner or in some alternate manner. If a recording of the old and the new procedures are played back, fruitful discussions about important elements may be held.

It is also sometimes valuable not to take up the time of the entire group in listening to a recording. The protagonist may listen to it alone or in company with his antagonist, with an observer, or in a small group. The performance can then be dissected at length.

Another valuable procedure is to have a discussion about certain critical areas, and then to replay the recording. Confrontation is a powerful tool. If a protagonist should deny a certain element (which, as we have pointed out is not unusual, because people just don't see and hear themselves) and then find out for himself by listening to the recording that the opinions of others are correct and that his own are wrong, this is usually a most effective learning situation.

A good example of this occurred with a supervisor who was told by the observers that he had a habit of not permitting people to finish their ideas—that he constantly interrupted them. He denied this vigorously, but when he listened to a tape recording he was astounded to discover that in more than 80 per cent of the thought exchanges, he did precisely this. He then argued that this was not unusual. However, when a number of other tapes were played back from a library of recordings of the very same situation, he found that the percentage of interruptions by others was far below the amount he indulged in. This was a much more meaningful lesson to him than any amount of discussion by others.

Techniques

IN ROLEPLAYING a subject enacts a role the way he usually plays it, would like to play it, or thinks he would play it while the antagonist acts as he conceives another would behave, or as he himself would in reality. But straight roleplaying is sometimes not sufficient to attain the director's purposes, so he uses any of a variety of special techniques to emphasize such elements as skill-development, insight, flexibility, empathy, generalizations, etc. Knowing when to use a particular special technique, and knowing how to put it into effective action is the hallmark of the capable director.

Structuring a Situation

Mr. Abt, a foreman in a training group, states he has trouble with Mr. Reb, his engineering supervisor. To find the nature of the problem, the discussion in the group might go somewhat as follows:

YEW: *(Director):* Well, tell us about this problem with Mr. Reb.
ABT: He doesn't seem to undestand me.

YEW: Can you give an example? *(Notice the director is interested at this point in a specific situation.)*

ABT: Like when I ask him for supplies . . .

YEW: Can you recall a specific instance? *(still pressing for a single illustrative situation.)*

ABT: Well, last week, we were running short of stock, and I asked him to get some more for me.

BAY: Couldn't you ask someone else?

YEW: Just a moment! We want to avoid that type of question. We are not interested here in alternate procedures, or better ways to handle a problem. What we want to see is how Mr. Abt deals with Mr. Reb. *(The director is alert to prevent any digression into nonessential areas, which may lead into free-for-all discussions.)*

ABT: No. He is the one I have to ask.

YEW: Abt, will you play your part and we shall try to get some one to play the part of Mr. Reb.

ABT: I guess anyone can do it.

YEW: It is usually best to get someone who looks like the person or acts like him, or has a personality something like his. Whom would you select out of the group?

ABT: I think Fee could do it. He looks and acts something like Mr. Reb.

YEW: Fine, do you accept the assignment, Mr. Fee?

FEE: O.K. But I don't know what it is all about.

YEW: Mr. Abt, will you please tell Mr. Fee about Mr. Reb and your problem?

ABT: It goes like this. I am the foreman and I have to supervise seven people. They ask me for materials. Some people get anxious unless they have a lot of stock, and I have to make sure they have enough to work with. But I can't requisition any without getting Mr. Reb's permission. And it is sometimes hard to get it. When I ask him, he sometimes says 'yes,' and sometimes 'no.' I never know what he will say, and when he says 'no,' he doesn't seem to listen to me.

YEW: How would you describe Mr. Reb in action?

ABT: Well, he is kind of bossy. He is an engineer and he thinks no one knows anything except himself.

YEW: I think we have enough to get started on. Where and when did this take place? *(Trying to get a specific instance.)*

ABT: Yesterday at the shop.

YEW: Where did you talk to him?

ABT: In his office.

YEW: How did it happen?

ABT: I met him in the corridor, and he told me to come into his office.

YEW: Did you sit down?

ABT: No. He only asked me what I wanted, and we talked standing up.

YEW: How long? *(Notice Yew asks short simple questions.)*

ABT: About two minutes.

YEW: Well, let us try to roleplay the situation just as it happened. Now, Abt, if Mr. Fee doesn't act just the way Mr. Reb acted, stop the action, and explain how he should act. Now, walk toward each other, from opposite sides of the room, and when you get in the middle Abt, stop Mr. Fee who is acting the role of Mr. Reb. Is that clear? Good. Now, one more thing, Abt. What was Mr. Reb's attitude about your request?

ABT: He said he'd look into it. He just stalled me.

YEW: Let's see what happened. As far as we know, Mr. Reb didn't agree with your request.

ABT: That's right.

YEW: O.K. Let us proceed. Will the others please observe Mr. Abt's behavior? Abt, stop the action the moment that Mr. Fee doesn't behave like Mr. Reb. *(Clap hands once to get things going. Mr. Yew has a signal: one clap means start; two claps mean stop.)*

Straight Roleplaying

(The two men start walking toward the center of the room.)

ABT (ABT): Oh, Mr. Reb. May I ask you a question?

FEE (REB): What is it?

ABT (ABT): We need some more stock. I'd like to get a requisition.

FEE (REB): Well, step in my office and tell me about it.

ABT (ABT): Thanks. *(Both men move as though into an office.)*

FEE (REB): What do you want?

ABT (ABT): Some more stock.

FEE (REB): You got a week's supply only a couple of days ago.

* * *

ABT: No. That's not the way he would say it. *(Interrupting the action.)*

83

YEW: What would he say?

ABT: He'd say what kind of stock? and what do you want it for?

YEW: O.K. Fee, ask him again what he wants.

*　*　*

FEE (REB): Well, what do you want this time? And what for?

ABT (ABT): More stock. We're short.

FEE (REB): What kind of stock?

ABT (ABT): Well, for the punch presses.

FEE (REB): You sure you need it?

ABT (ABT): I wouldn't be asking you if I didn't need it.

FEE (REB): Sometimes people ask for things they don't need.

ABT (ABT): Well, I need it. Why do I have to argue with you everytime I want something?

FEE (REB): You do your job and I'll do mine. I'll come over and look things over, and if you need it, then you'll get it.

*　*　*

YEW: *(Clapping hands twice):* Well, we got a small example of behavior. Is that how it goes, Abt?

ABT: Something like that. He is a hard man to deal with, never know how he'll react. Just isn't fair to me.

YEW: We aren't here to try to analyze or help Mr. Reb, we want to help you. Now, let's ask Mr. Fee how he felt about you. What impression did you get, Fee? *(Usually the first person to ask for an impression is the antagonist.)*

FEE: Well, I got the impression that Abt wasn't sure of himself, as though he felt I wouldn't give it to him. He has a kind of peculiar attitude. I don't know what to call it.

YEW: Would you have given him the stock if he had asked you in that way?

REB: I think he had an antagonistic attitude. I don't know what I would have done.

Rationale. Straight roleplaying permits observers to see the protagonist in normal action. Usually, the director lets a situation go on for at least five minutes to permit participants to warm up and to get over any stiffness. Because the situation is contrived, Mr. Abt is also able to watch himself in action more than in a real situation, where he would not be aware

84

of himself. Straight roleplaying is the most usual roleplaying technique and is the one commonly utilized for testing, training, and demonstration purposes.

Doubling

In real life we often "talk" to ourselves. In contemplating any course of action, or trying to figure out any problem we "discuss with ourselves" the pros and cons of any situation. Just as straight roleplaying concerns itself with a representation of action, the doubling technique is a representation of contemplation.

Example. Bay brings up a problem not readily dramatized, and the director decides to use the doubling procedure to obtain more information.

YEW: When we have a problem in our minds we usually try to think around it, see it from every point of view. Let us use the doubling technique here to explore Bay's problem. I think it would be best if I'd be Bay's double to let you see how it works. Now, this is the way it goes, Mr. Bay. I'll be your other self, and I'll think along with you. I'll imitate all your motions and actions and will try to think as you do. Now, let us sit up front here so everybody can see us, and you just think aloud about your problem.
(Both men sit down face-to-face and as the scene develops, Mr. Yew imitates Bay's behavior.)

❀ ❀ ❀

BAY (BAY): I wonder what I should do about my job.
YEW (BAY): I can't make up my mind.
BAY (BAY): There are a lot of possibilities.
YEW (BAY): For example . . .
BAY (BAY): Well, I could take the job in Burlington, but my wife wouldn't want to move.
YEW (BAY): I suppose she . . .
BAY (BAY): I think she just doesn't want to leave her family.
YEW (BAY): She just is set on staying here.
BAY (BAY): Yes, she is. But after all the opportunities are greater than in Auburn.

YEW (BAY): I don't think she understands that.

BAY (BAY): She understands that all right, she is just scared, that's what it is.

YEW (BAY): Just scared. I wonder if I am scared, too.

BAY (BAY): Yes, I suppose I am scared, too.

YEW (BAY): It's not only my wife that's scared, me too.

BAY (BAY): Well, I don't know how it will work out.

YEW (BAY): After all, it is a chance I'll have to take.

BAY (BAY): On the other hand, the possibilities are good. I don't want to be stuck here in Auburn the rest of my life.

YEW (BAY): I want to go and I don't want to go.

BAY (BAY): I do want to go. It's my wife who is putting doubts in me. I don't seem to be able to convince her.

YEW (BAY): On the other hand, I don't know if I am convinced myself.

BAY (BAY): I'm convinced. I know it is the right thing. I just can't convince her.

YEW (BAY): All I have to do is convince her and then I'll take the job.

BAY (BAY): Yes, that's all there is to it. I'll have to say to her, "Honey, I'm just going to take that job, that's all there is to it."

YEW (BAY): And she'll say . . .

BAY (BAY): "Are you sure you are doing the right thing? Suppose it doesn't work out?"

YEW (BAY): Then, I'll say, "We just have to take a chance. That's all there is to it."

BAY (BAY): That's what I'll tell her.

❋   ❋   ❋

YEW (*Clapping his hands twice*): Now, let us do some straight roleplaying. Let Bay take his own role and we'll get a wife for him from the group and let us see what will happen tonight when he comes home and tells his wife he has made up his mind. (*Men or women can readily take other-sex roles in roleplaying.*)

Rationale. Those familiar with Carl Rogers' psychotherapeutic technique, client-centered counseling, will realize that a close parallel exists between the procedure of doubling and the nondirective type of counseling. The double thinks along with the protagonist, raises questions and repeats ideas, but does not contradict the subject. The purpose of this procedure is not only to help the protagonist to understand himself—its major value—but also to give others insights into how the subject thinks before going into straight roleplaying. The antagonist who plays the role of the double should have a considerable amount of insight into human nature, and, as illustrated above, it is usually best for the director himself to play the double at least at first.

Switching

The most common roleplaying variation is switching or role-reversal. The protagonist takes the role of his antagonist. In this way he literally puts himself in the other's place, since not only does he now take on the antagonist's role, but he actually switches physically over to the antagonist's physical location, such as changing chairs, and continues from the interrupted point.

Example. Abt informs the group that he is having trouble with Cor, the man who shares his office. Mr. Dee, their mutual supervisor, will not adjust the situation. The director decides to have Abt visit 'Dee' to discuss the matter.

In reading the dialogue below, keep in mind that while the primary purpose of roleplaying in this case is diagnostic, to learn how Abt handles Dee, a secondary purpose may be for Abt to see a new solution to the problem. In differentiation to the case method which is concerned with solutions, roleplaying is primarily concerned with dynamics—the *how* rather than the *what*. Sometimes new solutions to problems do appear, as in this case.

ABT (ABT): Mr. Dee, I'd like to talk with you about something.
BAY (DEE): What is it, Mr. Abt? Won't you sit down?
ABT *(Breaking in):* No. That isn't the way Dee would say it. He is more curt.

87

DIRECTOR: Change seats. Now, Bay, you start just the way Abt did. Mr. Abt, you sit at the desk and now you're Mr. Dee. Let's start it over.

❊   ❊   ❊

BAY (ABT): Mr. Dee, I'd like to talk to you.
ABT (DEE): What is it this time?

❊   ❊   ❊

DIRECTOR: O.K., let us switch back and start it over.

❊   ❊   ❊

ABT (ABT): Mr. Dee, I'd like to see you.
BAY (DEE): What is it this time?
ABT (ABT): The same thing. The room.
BAY (DEE): What about it?
ABT (ABT): I hope you'll listen to me. I am only thinking of the company's welfare, and nothing else. I have to read reports, memoranda, and I have to do a great deal of writing. Now, Cor bothers me. I have nothing against him personally, you know, it is only that his voice bothers me. He has a loud voice and he is always on the telephone and when he talks it distracts me.

❊   ❊   ❊

DIRECTOR: Switch. *(The roleplayers change seats.)*

❊   ❊   ❊

BAY (ABT): I want to do my job but I just can't seem to concentrate when Cor talks. That's the whole story.
ABT (DEE): Have you talked with Cor about it? He is a reasonable man.

❊   ❊   ❊

DIRECTOR: Switch. *(Note that Abt [Dee] asks Bay [Abt] a question which only the real Abt can answer, so the director makes a switch.)*

❊   ❊   ❊

88

ABT (ABT): No, I haven't.

BAY (DEE): Why not?

ABT (ABT): Well, I don't want to antagonize him. I figure he may not like it. It may sound like a criticism.

BAY (DEE): Well, it seems to me that seems like the best solution. Talk to him.

＊　＊　＊

DIRECTOR: Switch again.

＊　＊　＊

ABT (DEE): Just talk to Cor. I'm sure he'll be reasonable.

BAY (ABT): But you don't understand. I can't do it.

ABT (DEE): Just talk to him. What do you want me to do?

BAY (ABT): Change our rooms.

ABT (DEE): You know we can't do that!

BAY (ABT): Why not?

ABT (DEE): There is no place. We'll have to think of another solution. Don't you have any? Something practical?

BAY (ABT): Well, if he could schedule his phone calls so that there would be a minimum of interference, that might be a solution.

＊　＊　＊

DIRECTOR: Switch again, please.

＊　＊　＊

ABT (ABT): But I don't know whether he can do that. Besides, there are a lot of incoming calls.

BAY (DEE): How about one of those gadgets that go on the phone and one can whisper into it?

ABT (ABT): I don't know whether he would use it.

BAY (DEE): Suppose I tell him to use it?

ABT (ABT): Then he'd know that I complained.

BAY (DEE): What's wrong with that?

ABT (ABT): Well, I don't like to get into trouble with him.

Rationale. From this short account it is evident that by switching Abt from the role of himself to that of Dee his supervisor, he gets experience in seeing things from the other's point of view. This technique can be extremely powerful, and is especially valuable in cases of frozen thinking, when the protagonist is absolutely convinced of the wrongness of another person's point of view, intentions, etc. In some dramatic cases, the clever director working with an involved individual can help him to gain immediate insight into the untenability of his own strongly held position.

The logic for the use of switching is that in frozen thinking one can only see one's own point of view. By putting the protagonist in a position where he is forced to think like his antagonist, he may now be able to see both sides. The antagonist who now takes on the role of the protagonist should imitate the protagonist in his voice, language, and actions.

Imitation Technique

This important technique is designed to give individuals an understanding of how others see them. The poet Robert Burns was talking about the imitation technique when he wrote, "O, wad some pow'r the giftie gie us, to see oursels as ithers see us," because this is precisely what this procedure accomplishes. The subject in this technique sits in the audience. He watches another person play him on the "stage" and so in this manner can see himself—as in a mirror, so to speak.

Example. Fee, a foreman, complains that his subordinates seem to mock him. They appear to have an antagonistic attitude toward him, and he cannot seem to impress them. He just cannot understand their behavior, and he has experimented with a variety of manners of dealing with them, but without success. This is a serious problem for him, and already his own supervisor has commented on the relatively poor attitude his men seem to have toward him.

Let us say that the director has Fee act out a typical situation by straight roleplaying with an employee-surrogate. We then have Fee (Fee) versus Abt (Zin). The observers look on and obtain an impression of how Fee affects Zin. The problem is how to get Fee to see and understand how he acts—how he appears to others. A variety of techniques can be used for this purpose. For example, the director could stop the session and initiate a discussion; or, he could use role-reversal with Fee (Zin) versus Abt (Fee). In this way Fee, acting the role of his own subordinate can see how Zin, the supervisor, is affected by Fee. By using the imitation technique, he may ask a member of the observing group to duplicate Fee's behavior. Now, Cor (Fee) acts versus Abt (Zin). Cor attempts to play the role just the way that Fee did. In this manner, Fee, sitting in the audience, sees himself as others see him.

Rationale. Let us give a simple but appropriate analogy. A man is walking along a street, hurrying to work, when he notices that people seem to be looking at him. He glances at his clothes: his shoes match, and so do his trousers and jacket. He can see nothing wrong. He stops in front of a mirror and sees that he has a streak of soot along his brow. In looking in the mirror he sees himself as others see him, and he now can understand others' reactions to him.

It is difficult to believe how wrong people can be about themselves. None of us can really see ourselves as others see us—and ordinarily, we strongly reject critical opinions. Critical opinions usually come from those close to us—wives, mothers, children, friends—whose judgment we do not trust, thinking them biased, or as having too high standards, being overcritical, etc. It is one of the requirements of roleplaying that other members be seen as neutral. Then, the role being played on the stage is accepted by the protagonist as representative of himself. Nevertheless, it is common experience for the subject of the imitation technique to complain that the imitation of himself is a caricature—a crude distortion—he just cannot be so bad! At this point the director implements the imitation technique by asking various members to comment on how true-to-life the imitation was. The poor subject is usually surprised to learn how others see him, but inevitably, he returns again to the stage in an attempt to unfreeze his behavior. Once again, after a new version, the imitation technique may be used to show him how he has changed. Frequent discussions and evaluations usually accompany the employment of the imitation technique.

Private Thoughts

In any human interaction, individuals usually communicate ideas and feelings. How valid are these communications? Often there is a close connection between what one says and what one thinks and feels, but in some cases the correspondence is not at all close. If Abt, Bay's supervisor, tends to shout, it is not very likely that Bay will say "Look, I don't like you shouting at me." What he says and what he feels may be two quite different things.

A method of informing people how they affect others is the private thoughts technique, which when well employed can contribute greatly to a subject's self-understanding.

Example. Let us take the example of Fee as explained above in the mirror technique. He did not seem to impress his subordinates favorably, but he had no idea what was wrong—how they really felt—or what caused them to feel this way.

Fee acts himself in straight roleplaying versus an antagonist who takes the role of a subordinate. The straight roleplaying involved Fee (Fee) the foreman, versus Abt (Zin) an employee. Abt has acted the role he thinks a subordinate would act in the situation. Let us assume that Fee agrees that Abt's

92

portrayal is correct. Now, the director asks Bay to speak Zin's inner thoughts. The director says to Bay, "Stand behind Mr. Abt, who is playing the role of Zin. Abt will respond with the replies that he believes Zin will make; but you are to speak what Zin is *really* thinking. Put your hand on Mr. Abt's shoulders when you want to talk. And now, Mr. Abt, let us suppose that Mr. Bay does speak out your thoughts and feelings as you act with Mr. Fee, then do nothing—but if he should not express your real feelings, stop the action and tell Mr. Bay what you do feel."

FEE (FEE): Look, Zin, I want to talk to you.

ABT (ZIN): Yes, sir. [BAY (ZIN'): What is on his mind now?]

FEE (FEE): We have a rush order, and I have to go over to another department, and when I come back I want you to have that job completed.

ABT (ZIN): I'll get to it right away. [BAY (ZIN'): Why does he shout at me? I don't like how he talks.]

FEE (FEE): Do you think you can do it in time?

ABT (ZIN): When will you get back? [BAY (ZIN'): How am I supposed to know when he's coming back?]

FEE (FEE): You know it takes me an hour or so when I'm at the drafting department.

ABT (ZIN): Yes, sir. [BAY (ZIN'): How on earth was I supposed to know what department he was going to go to? That's the way he is. He gives me a bit of information, and he thinks I know what's in his mind. Besides, he's got a nasty way of talking to me. I don't like it a bit. I have some self-respect. I'd like to talk to him about it someday.]

ABT (ZIN): Should I ask any of the others to help me? I don't know if I can get it done in time.

FEE (FEE): I could do it in a half hour. [BAY (ZIN'): Like hell you could.]

ABT (ZIN): O.K., I'll work on it as hard as I can. I hope nothing else will come up.

FEE (FEE): Just do this, nothing else. [BAY (ZIN'): So if there is an emergency or something, all I have to say is that Fee told me to do nothing else. Would he stick by me? Probably not.]

93

Rationale. This inner thoughts technique is based on the concept that there is often discrepancy between what a person does and says and what that person really thinks and feels. In life, with its emphasis on courtesy and tact, people frequently act nicely to others to their face, but may take them apart in private. If supervisors could overhear employees discussing them, some might be terribly shocked. The Private Thoughts technique helps a person eavesdrop on others, and gives protagonists an understanding of the effect that they make on other people.

It is of interest to note that most often the antagonist will support the validity of the person who plays the part of his own inner thoughts, and frequently he is surprised how well this other person can understand him.

The Wheel

The roleplaying director is a creative artist. He is able to use not only the more-or-less standard techniques, but can also devise situations to meet special needs. The technique described below, which can be called the Wheel, because the single antagonist, sitting in the middle of the circle of group members, becomes the hub of the situation, is an example of an alternate technique.

The members were salesmen, and the director (who will also play the role of the antagonist) asked the following question of the group: "What statement made to you by prospects is the most difficult for you to handle?" A number of statements were suggested, and two seemed to have general meaning: "We don't think we can use the services of your organization" and "We don't think we can afford it."

The director now sat in the center of the circled group and

said: "Let us suppose that you are trying to sell me, and I shall make this statement in turn, to each of you: "I am sorry, but I don't think we can use your service, and besides, we cannot afford it." Now, as soon as I make the statement, respond to it in the best way you can."

A tape recorder was turned on, and the wheel-situation went something as follows:

YEW *(to Abt):* I am sorry but I don't think we can use your service, and besides we cannot afford it.

ABT: A number of our satisfied customers felt just as you did at first, but on deciding to experiment, they were satisfied that we had something to offer.

YEW *(to Bay):* I don't think we need your services, and besides we cannot afford them.

BAY: I see your point of view, and it would be the reaction that I would have myself perhaps on first hearing about it, but if I may show you some additional material, I think you will change your mind.

YEW *(to Cor):* I am sorry, but I don't think we can afford it, and I don't see that we need your services.

COR: Your competition sees the value of this service, and they have considered it carefully. What may seem at first as something perhaps not too useful will become, in your mind, something much more valuable as time goes on.

YEW *(to Dee):* No. I don't think I need or can afford your service.

DEE: You are a progressive manager, and from your past efforts it is evident that you will not make a summary decision without a consideration of all the facts. I wonder if we couldn't meet again in a week or so to discuss this.

YEW *(to Ego):* I don't think we can use your services and I doubt we can afford them.

EGO: I can understand your point of view, but I want to assure you that I have studied the needs of your company, and I believe that in a very short time the advantages of this program will become evident to you if you decide to try it.

YEW *(to Fee):* I can't see we need it or can afford it.

FEE: Now, in your company you have a problem with other employees. I can show you in a moment's time how this program will help them.

95

After the wheel was completed, each person saying what he thought might be the best response, each statement was replayed from the recording machine. After each statement the various members commented in terms of the suitability of the various ideas, which were then put on a blackboard. Finally, on the basis of a discussion, some of the less effective replies were eliminated, and generalized proper answers were developed. Then, the wheel was again resorted to, and now the replies ran somewhat as follows:

YEW *(to Abt):* I don't think we can afford your program, and I doubt we need it.

ABT: I understand and appreciate your point of view, sir. I have no desire to try to change your mind in any way. As a matter of fact if we were not to be useful to you, we wouldn't want you to invest in this program. However, may I point out that you have a particular problem in your company, which other companies also have—your older men do not know what to do about retirement. Now, we have developed a program dealing directly with this situation, which I would like to show you.

YEW *(to Bay):* I don't think we can afford or that we really need your program.

BAY: Mr. Marx, in the Alpha Company, also thought the same when I first talked to him, but he was willing to give us a chance to demonstrate what we could do, and if you wish to call him up, I am certain that he would tell you that we are saving him a lot of money and are giving him a most valuable service.

YEW *(to Cor):* I don't think we need or can afford your service.

COR: Yes, it is frequently hard to see the need for a new service, but very often needs creep up on us which require new ways of thinking out problems and handling them. Now, we have developed a program that meets a common problem which I know affects you, and if I may show you some data I think it may interest you.

Rationale. The wheel technique is one which usually causes a great deal of interest when properly employed—which should be in a situation where every member has the same problem. Each individual shows how he would handle a unit situation, and then by playback and discussion, errors in general presen-

96

tations can be located and eliminated, and better responses can be substituted. It is useful in using this technique, not only to depend on the consensus of opinions of members, but to have an expert who serves as an observer and judge, who can help formulate a final presentation. The presentation, as was evident from the second go-around need not be stereotyped.

Substitution

This technique has not yet been described in the literature, but comes from a personal communication with Boris Speroff, one of the more prolific writers in this field.

The substitution technique is very much like the switching technique, except now the antagonist is switched. Thus, if Abt is the protagonist and is playing himself against Bay who is playing the role of Zin, by substituing Cor in the role of Zin, we can now demonstrate to Abt how different people will elicit different reactions from Abt. This may be called for when Abt thinks he generally acts in a constant manner, when the truth is that how he acts with people depends on how they act toward him. For example, let us say that Abt insists he is always very polite to people, and then Bay and Cor are asked to act in different ways. Short transcriptions of how Abt actually reacted to Bay and Cor may be indicated here.

I A

ABT: This is the third time this week I told you to watch out for this particular error.

BAY: Yes, sir. I don't know how it happened.

ABT: Well, watch yourself from now on.

I B

ABT: This is the third time this week I told you to watch out for this particular error.

COR: It isn't my fault.

ABT: Well, it isn't my fault either you know.

97

II A

ABT: From now on before you go ahead, ask me what you should do.
BAY: O.K., sir, I'll do just that.
ABT: That's the spirit.

II B

ABT: From now on before you go ahead, ask me what you should do.
COR: You mean I'll have to ask you every time?
ABT: You heard me. I say what I mean.

III A

ABT: We can't afford such mistakes any more.
COR: You're right, I'll do my best.
ABT: That's the spirit.

III B

ABT: We can't afford such mistakes any more.
COR: You'd think I was the only one making mistakes.
ABT: You just do what you are told to do, and none of your smart remarks.

Rationale. People often don't realize the nature of human interactions—how one person can affect another. If any protagonist tries to play himself against another who varies, he must adjust to the situation. The substitution technique is an effective procedure for showing how individuals are not constant in their dealing with others.

Variations and Combinations

In this section we shall discuss some combinations and variations of roleplaying. These are limited only by the imagination of the director.

98

Multiple Roleplaying

This variation introduced by Maier (53) consists essentially of having a large group broken into small groups, each group enacting the same situation simultaneously. Ordinarily, those in the small groups have their parts outlined by means of printed directions. One of the group may serve as an observer, who later reports to the total group what happened in his own subgroup. The director may have a chart or outline form on which he can indicate various actions taken.

IDEAS Technique

This procedure combines lecturing, demonstrating and multiple roleplaying. The "I" stands for *Introduction,* and usually is a lecture by the director. Then follows a *Demonstration.* Previously prepared individuals act out a demonstration problem before the whole group. The demonstration obviates the need for written directions, since the rest of the group learn the problem by watching and listening. The third phase is Multiple Roleplaying, and is labeled *Enactment.* The whole group is broken into subgroups usually including one or two observers, and the people in the subgroups multiple roleplay the problem outlined in the demonstration. Then comes *Action.* This is a single roleplaying, repeating performances before the entire group by one or more of the smaller groups—selecting the roleplaying groups on the basis of reports by the observers. Finally comes the *Summary,* at which time the Director lectures, attempting to summarize the meaning of the session. (21)

This technique, as may be seen, calls for the director to serve as an authority. He actually does little roleplaying directing, since the Demonstration should either be prearranged or else may require people to read scripts. One interesting feature of this technique is that it is spindle-shaped: first and last comes the director-lecturer. In the second and fourth phases there is a single roleplaying, the first time in a nonspontaneous manner and the second time in a repeat performance. The middle phase is multiple roleplaying, and involves everyone.

On-the-Spot Roleplaying

Generally, we think of roleplaying as occurring in a private protected location. On-the-spot roleplaying calls for roleplaying in real situations. Essentially, the individual who is to roleplay is asked to act his part in reality, and this represents nothing more or less than reality try-out. For example, if a store manager were to ask a salesgirl applicant who claims store-selling experience, to go behind a counter and wait on a customer, while the manager observes her, we may call this on-the-spot roleplaying. The girl's behavior is, as far as the customer goes, not unusual. The customer, serving as the antagonist, may have no realization of the role she is playing. The store manager is the observer who watches how the girl operates in a reality situation.

Veridical Roleplaying

This is a variation of on-the-spot roleplaying, and calls for people to act reality roles for the purpose of understanding another's role. To give an example: a sales manager supervising other salesmen may periodically assume the role of a salesman and go in the field to test for himself how customers react to particular sales presentations or various products.

Advertising men may try to sell products to get the "feel" of peoples' attitudes to certain presentations; a superior may take a subordinate's role to understand that individual's problems.

The veridical roleplayer acts a role foreign to him to understand how the real individual who is to act the role in real life finds it; or how others react to particular situations.

100

APPLICATIONS

Training

TRAINING IS the most provocative and challenging area for roleplaying. Changes in human behavior are frequently the keys to decreased costs, increased productivity, and effective upgrading of performance in industrial organizations.

The limitations of information-giving whether by lecture, printed material, or other means to produce changes in behavior have already been discussed in Chapter 2. Whenever well-established patterns of behavior need to be changed, information-giving falls short of the goal. Bradford sums up contemporary thinking on this question:

> Let me offer one basic criterion we can use in testing any training or management development program. The fundamental goal of any program is to bring about a change in behavior. . . . We cannot be content with the assumption that learning information necessarily leads towards behavioral change in the way an individual actually performs back on the job. . . . Information and knowledge may lead to a shift in attitudes, but do not necessarily lead toward behavioral improvement.

To take a tough-minded, dollars-and-cents approach to management we cannot be content with less than improvement back on the job.[1]

Training Objectives

The basic objective of training is to change behavior or improve performance. Within this broad objective three subgoals may be defined. The first of these is *training in methods*. There are a great many tasks in industry which require specific skills and techniques. For example, operators in a mass production factory frequently must learn the step-by-step methods involved in doing a particular job. Supervisors who train production workers must be taught job instruction training methods. Interviewing, conference leadership, salesmanship, and many other necessary skills in industry require knowledge of and the ability to use specific techniques and methods. In any training situation where the emphasis is on teaching an established pattern of procedures, the approach is essentially *method-centered.*

In addition to mastering established methods of procedure, it is necessary in many training situations for participants to learn how to handle variations in problem situations. Thus, in some sessions the focus is on problems rather than on methods. The approach is essentially *problem-centered.*

Finally there are requirements that trainees increase self-understanding. Such sessions deal with individual insights and personal effectiveness. The approach is *individual-centered.*

Method-centered Roleplaying

A good example of method-centered training is provided by the JIT (Job Instruction Training) Program developed by the War Manpower Commission during World War II. The

1. Leland P. Bradford, "A look at management growth and development." *Journal of the American Society of Training Directors,* 1958, 12 (7), 4.

program focused on teaching well-established patterns for training new employees. It was designed primarily for supervisors who were faced with the tremendous task of training a great number of marginal members of the labor market who entered defense industries during the war. The goal of JIT was to provide supervisors with a step-by-step outline for instructing new employees. The four steps which are the core of Job Instruction Training are: (1) Prepare the worker; (2) Present the operation; (3) Try-out performance; (4) Follow-up. The JIT program was comprised of a series of demonstrations and lectures on how to accomplish these four steps, but the emphasis of the program was on developing effectiveness in implementing the four-step process. Here is an example of a typical JIT roleplaying session:

*(The roleplayers are two members of a supervisory group, both of whom are being trained to instruct new employees. One supervisor plays his own role as a trainer and the other plays the role of a new worker. For purposes of illustration, step 2 of the JIT process will be used, that is—*present the operation.)

SUPERVISOR: All right John, now that you know a little bit about the set-up here and I've shown you how your work place is laid out, let's go over your job, step-by-step. Feel free to interrupt me at any time and to ask me any questions that occur to you. Now I don't want you to worry if you don't get this the first time. We'll just take our time and keep at it until I'm able to make it clear. Now the first thing you do is pick up this housing, and place it in this jig right in front of you. Is that clear?

EMPLOYEE: Yes.

SUPERVISOR: Now, with your right hand you pick up a bolt from this tray and at the same time with your left hand pick up a nut from the tray on your left. Now one thing to remember at this point is when you're picking up the bolt always pick it up by the head. This will save you time, and you won't have to turn the bolt over in your hand and it is ready to insert in the housing. Now place the bolt in the housing with your right hand and bring the nut up from below with your left and just tighten it finger-tight. Just two turns is all that is needed.

104

The supervisor then continues going through the job step-by-step calling the worker's attention to key points that should be remembered. When the entire presentation of the operation has been made the trainer stops the action and solicits comments from the group. The discussion goes something like this:

TRAINER: Now, in previous sessions we've discussed this job and broken it down: You each have a job break-down which shows the steps and key points in carrying out the job. Do you have any comments on how this operation was presented to the worker?

PARTICIPANT A: Yes, the supervisor left out a key point right at the start. He should have told the worker to place the housing with the flat surface in front. This is an important key point, because if the worker doesn't do it this way he will have to turn the housing around and will be wasting time.

TRAINER *(addressing the supervisor who had been playing his own role):* How does that comment check out with your break-down of how the job should be presented?

SUPERVISOR: Yes, I'm afraid I left that key point out. I agree it should be in the break-down of the job.

TRAINER: OK, well, you'll notice that it takes almost a full second for the worker to turn the housing around if he doesn't place it properly to begin with, so you can see that when a man is turning out four or five hundred of these pieces a day, one second per piece can amount to a lot of wasted time. I'm glad this came up because it shows how important some minor key point can be in helping the new worker get started on the right foot. Any other comments?

PARTICIPANT B: Yes, I noticed that the instructor forgot to tell the employee that he should always place the first bolt in the outer right hand hole in the housing. If he doesn't do this he will get in trouble when he gets farther along in assembling the part.

This somewhat oversimplified illustration shows how a method-centered roleplaying approach can be utilized. Trainees are provided with an opportunity to try out their own effectiveness in instructing others and receive straightforward guidance based upon a well-established pattern of job instruction. Successful training occurs when participants are able to go through an entire instruction situation covering all four basic steps in teaching the job in a systematic and clear way.

Problem-centered Roleplaying

A Job Instruction Training situation can also be used to illustrate problem-centered training:

Frequently job instruction techniques are utilized in training experienced employees who have developed poor work habits or those who are asked to change their methods of doing the job. In these situations step-by-step methods of proceeding are not sufficient to accomplish successful instruction. When the supervisor attempts to apply straight JIT with experienced workers he finds that it frequently does not "take." Therefore, the supervisor must not only be trained in JIT methods, but also must develop understanding and insight concerning the experienced worker's feelings and attitudes. The following example concerns a group of supervisors being trained in how to instruct experienced workers in a change in job methods: (After some warm-up and discussion a roleplaying situation is structured in which one supervisor plays his own role and a second supervisor plays the role of an experienced worker. The man in the role of the worker may either be orally briefed by the supervisor, or a written briefing, which brings out key problems, may be prepared in advance by the trainer.)

SUPERVISOR: Good morning, Bill, I've got something I'd like to talk to you about.

BILL: OK, what's up?

SUPERVISOR: Well, Bill, you've been doing a fine job and you really turn out a lot of production. We've got something that I think is going to make your job easier and make it possible for you to get your job done with a little less effort. We've had a group of time study engineers studying the job that you and the rest of the fellows on this floor are doing, and they've come up with a method which is really going to save you time. Let me show you how it works.

(*The foreman might then go on demonstrating the new operation.*)

106

BILL: Look, I've been doing this job for about six months, and I've gotten to the point where it's almost automatic with me. I turn out as much work as anyone else and I'm really pretty satisfied with the way things are going.

SUPERVISOR: Believe me, Bill, I wouldn't be asking you to change your method if I wasn't sure that this new approach was really better.

BILL: Well, it may be better but it took me a couple of months to catch on to this way of doing it and I had to work like hell for awhile in order to meet production. If I change methods now it will mean going through that all over again. I can't see any advantage in that.

Here, the supervisor is faced with a somewhat different problem from that in the first situation. Bill is so resistant to the new idea that there is no step-by-step method for resolving the conflict. The problem-centered approach to roleplaying is now appropriate. In essence this involves experimentation by group members with various ways of handling the conflict situation, and the development of alternate courses of action which seem appropriate. The focus of this session is on increasing the participant's understanding of the total situation and providing him with an opportunity to improve his skills in resolving such conflicts. It can be readily observed that although this is a problem in Job Instruction Training, it may be generalized into many other areas. It is in some ways similar to the problem of the salesman faced with the customer who is not ready to buy. It has ingredients present in a great many interpersonal situations involving supervisors, salesmen, staff men, union officials, and so on.

It is not enough to tell a salesman that he must smile, get the prospect's attention, talk briefly about something the prospect is interested in, talk benefits, and follow certain established procedures for closing the sale. The salesman must learn to deal with dynamic situations and with a variety of people whose feelings and attitudes are paramount in determining the salesman's effectiveness. An interviewer can be taught to follow a pattern of questions but his ability to perceive and understand the feelings of the interviewee, his ability to establish rapport and really listen with understanding provide a much greater challenge. An executive can be taught a great deal about planning, systems, controls, motivation theory, and so on. In the executive situation perhaps more than in any other industrial role, the ability to administer and to adjust to change is most highly valued. Problem-centered roleplaying can be used effectively to deal with these kinds of situations. Its major advantage is that it is not stereotyped, that results are not predetermined, and that it is, in essence, action training in becoming more effective. It can be used in practically any situation where a training group faces reasonably common problems which cannot be resolved with pat answers. If there is a "one best way" of handling a situation, then the training may consist of a lecture, written presentation, or method-centered roleplaying to get across the "one best way." When the focus of the training session is on dealing with a complex social situation where "right answers" are not immediately available then the trainer must use a developmental approach. Problem-centered roleplaying is developmental training and meets this need.

In problem-centered sessions, the roleplaying enactment should be kept on the level of a general problem rather than on a personal or personality level. When one deals with an individual's personal problems in handling a given situation the session becomes "individual-centered." This is not to say that in a problem-centered session individual insights are not developed. Certainly participants may increase their individual effectiveness and learn something about their own personality. The point is, however, that the problem-centered session is primarily concerned with skills, and not personality difficulties.

Individual-centered Roleplaying

A job instruction training situation will again be used to illustrate individual-centered roleplaying:

An office supervisor in an industrial plant has an unusually high rate of turnover in his department. Investigation discloses his subordinates to be poorly trained and to have a negative attitude toward their boss and the company. Termination interviews reveal that employees feel that the supervisor is curt and tactless. In a roleplaying session, role reversal and the mirror technique, described in previous chapters, can be used to increase the supervisor's awareness of the effect of his behavior on others. As his awareness increases, he becomes encouraged to experiment with new approaches.

Integration of Roleplaying Approaches

The three illustrations above point up the differences in focus in method-centered, problem-centered, and individual-centered roleplaying sessions. Actually, all three approaches may be used in any given session. Thus, the roleplaying director may begin a session on a method-centered basis. He may find that although trainees follow a given step-by-step procedure quite closely they are unable to handle situations which depart from the established pattern. He may then switch to a more experimental method in which various approaches are tested and evaluated with emphasis on developing flexibility and sensitivity in handling the problem. Or he may find personal and attitudinal blocks which must be dealt with before either methods or skills can be developed. The director deals with whatever is present in the situation; that is, he deals with the here and now.

Two Key Areas

It follows from the foregoing discussion that roleplaying may be applied to a wide range of situations. In this and previous chapters, examples have been cited which illustrate roleplaying uses in safety, supervisory, methods, sales, and other training areas. However, there are two rather broad areas in which roleplaying is particularly suitable. The first is human relations training, the second, management and executive training. Because of the almost universal use of roleplaying in human relations training and its peculiar suitability for executive training, these two areas will be considered in some detail.

Human Relations

The use of the term *human relations* to describe a particular training area is somewhat misleading, for human relations are involved in almost every training situation. Nevertheless, in many training programs a series of sessions are devoted specifically to human relations principles and skills. Roleplaying brings an impact and intensity to these sessions which can rarely be duplicated by other techniques. Its use in human relations sessions fit into three general categories:

1. Training in the understanding and utilization of human relations principles.
2. Training in the knowledge and use of human relations skills.
3. Training in spontaneity[2].

---

2. Spontaneity training will be dealt with in Chapter X.

Training in Principles

An intellectual understanding of human relations can be communicated through lectures or other information-giving techniques. However, roleplaying can be used to change or at least lay the foundation for changing attitudes. Thus roleplaying can transform a purely instructional session into a more significant learning experience in which the trainee becomes deeply involved. For example, a trainer may try to get across the principle that "behavior is caused." The trainer might lecture on the subject explaining the stimulus-response idea, frustration-aggression hypothesis or other theoretical material. Or, he might structure a roleplaying sequence which would illustrate the principle and produce involvement on the part of participants. In this case rather than merely communicating information the trainer would provide an opportunity for exposure of attitudes and behavior and feedback of reactions.

Example. Although a foreman is used in the key role in the following instance of such a session, the case could easily be changed to cover office supervisors, managers, salesmen, or others.

A training group is informed they are about to witness interviews between a supervisor and three of his subordinates. The supervisor is to ask the subordinate to stay overtime to handle a rush order. The group is asked to watch the behavior of the subordinate and the boss in each of the interviews. They are to look for differences in the way the subordinates act and try to figure out why these differences exist. They are also to watch the boss and see if his reactions seem to change in each of the interviews and if so, why. (Trainer might supply the group with observer sheets or check lists on which to identify their reactions.)

Each of the roleplayers is given a written role which provides him with background information and a point of view on the problem. The three subordinates are asked to leave the room and re-enter one at a time so that they are not influenced by the interview preceding their own.

The roles supplied to the players can be as complicated as the trainer feels is necessary; however, for purposes of this illustration, fairly simple and brief roles will be used:

ROLE I

Sam Jones, Production Supervisor: You are about fifty and you have been with this company 27 years. Your boss just told you that a rush order has come in and you will have to stay tonight and get it out. It will be necessary for you to ask three of your men to work overtime. You have called the men and they are on their way to your office. One of the things which annoys you about this situation is that there have been 3 rush orders in the last ten days. As far as you are concerned, this is just a result of poor planning on the part of the Production Control Department. You had made plans to play bridge with friends tonight, so you know your wife is going to be annoyed. You'll have to call her and tell her you won't be home. Another thing that bothers you is that you know your men aren't going to like this or, at least, some of them won't. They like the money that comes from working overtime, but they like to know enough in advance so that they can make plans.

Because you are a foreman you don't get paid for the overtime at all and these guys are really getting a much better break than you are. Actually, the operators' overtime plus their base wages will bring their pay up to almost the same as yours. You have the responsibility of the whole department, you work more hours than anyone in it but the pay differential is pretty small. Nevertheless, there are still some advantages in being the boss.

ROLE II

Bill Thompson, Lathe Operator: You have worked for this company for about three years but you were just transferred to this department about three months ago. Actually, you don't know this foreman too well. You know he is going to ask you to work overtime and you do have a date tonight. You would like to try to talk your way out of the overtime assignment but you don't want to push it too hard because you had better start off on the right foot

112

with this new boss of yours. You are ambitious and you want the foreman to have a good opinion of you so if you find that he is pretty firm on the problem, you will probably go along with him. You don't mind getting that extra money for overtime. The main thing is that you want the foreman to think of you as a good employee.

ROLE III

Fred Jenkins, Drill Press Operator: You have worked here for quite a few years. You have always found this foreman to be a good Joe. Your wife just went out and bought some new furniture and you are a little bit in the hole. You want all the overtime you can get.

ROLE IV

Phil Streeter, Lathe Operator: You have been with this company about 15 years and you have always done a good job. You would like to get to be an assistant foreman; in fact, there was an opening in another department not long ago and you made a try for it. You heard through the grapevine that your boss wouldn't recommend you for the job. You really would like to start looking somewhere else for a new job but you have so much seniority with this company you aren't sure it would be a wise move. You figure you will work your eight hours and mind your own business.

The only satisfaction left for you around here is the bowling team. You have been in the league for quite a few years and really enjoy the game. Tonight your team is in the league playoff and you want to be there.

After having warmed up the group and the individual players to the problem, the separate interviews are conducted. They are limited to about five minutes each (or less) and are uninterrupted.

Upon completion of the interviews, the trainer guides the group in a discussion and analysis. He might begin by asking the group: "Did you notice much difference in the way the employees responded to the foreman?" As differences are brought out and discussed, the trainer can encourage the group to analyze why these differences existed. He can check their reactions with the players themselves. For example, the group might agree that the last player was rather negative and hostile toward the foreman. The trainer can then ask that player whether this was true. The questioning might be something like this:

TRAINER: The group seemed to think you were a little annoyed with the foreman, is that true?

PLAYER: Well, for one thing, I've got a bowling tournament tonight and I don't want to work.

TRAINER: Then the reason you were annoyed was that you didn't want to miss the bowling tournament. *(Turning to group)* Does this seem to explain what you saw?

The group then discusses whether this explains the foreman's behavior and they analyze and dig a little deeper to look for other causes for his reaction. Gradually they discover his underlying resentment toward his boss.

The group can then be encouraged to take a look at the foreman's responses.

The trainer can assist the group in synthesizing the results of their discussion and observation. As tentative conclusions are drawn, they can be tied in with the specific incidents which occurred during the roleplaying enactment. By the time the session ends the group is almost sure to agree that the behavior and responses of their subordinates are caused by a variety of factors. There will be an opportunity to discuss various causal factors, such as the personality and temperament of the individual, his past experience with his boss and with the company, and the forces and pressures acting on him at the time the interview occurs.

Thus, although a lecture could have been used to teach supervisors about this particular aspect of human relations, a roleplaying enactment brought drama and involvement to the learning situation. A theoretical concept can, in this way, take on real meaning and provide the basis for subsequent changes in attitude and behavior.

Training in Human Relations Skills

Human relations skills have attracted the attention of increasing numbers of industrial trainers. The ability to motivate subordinates, resolve conflicts and handle a variety of personnel problems is, at least to some extent, dependent upon the development and utilization of basic social skills. Roleplaying nicely suits these kinds of training sessions.

A typical area in human relations programs is training in "listening" skills. Counseling, interviewing, and other interpersonal techniques require the ability to listen with understanding.

Using two of the roles (Role I and Role IV) from the case shown above, roleplaying to train participants in listening skills can be demonstrated:

Three group members are assigned to the roles. One takes the part of the foreman (Role I), two other members take the part of the operator (Role IV) who does not want to work overtime. The trainer describes the setting and background of the case to the group. The two players who have been assigned the part of the subordinate are now asked to leave the room.

The group and the remaining roleplayer (Role I) briefly discuss how they feel the foreman should approach the operator. The purpose of this brief discussion is twofold: 1) to warmup the group to the problem, and 2) to remove the onus of possible failure from the individual playing the foreman's role, in that, since the foreman is being guided by the group in how to handle the interview, he is not personally at fault if the interview is unsuccessful.

The first "operator" is now called in and a brief uninterrupted interview takes place.

Rather than permitting the group to analyze and criticize the person playing the boss's role, the group members are asked to suggest how more information and understanding concerning the subordinates' point of view can be developed. For example, a group member might suggest: "I think the foreman should have given Phil (Role IV) more chance to talk." The trainer responds: "You feel *we* should have told the foreman to get Phil talking more." As the brief discussion continues the trainer quickly summarizes the suggestions. He then asks the "foreman" to try to incorporate these suggestions in the second interview. The second role player (Role IV) is then called into the room and a second, and longer, interview is conducted. When the interview is completed, suggestions are again solicited as to how the problem could be handled more effectively. Again the trainer stresses that the responsibility for the way in which the interview is handled is shared among group members. If time permits, additional approaches based upon group members suggestions are experimented with. Comments which are particularly perceptive are discussed in detail. For example, a group member might say: "I think that Phil was getting a little uncomfortable toward the end of the last interview. I noticed that he kept avoiding eye contact with the foreman." This observation is discussed and the trainer points out that communication is not just words but that tone, expression, and other minimal cues must be "listened for." Thus, through experimentation with various approaches to the problem of understanding the subordinate and by comparison and discussion of various perceptions and points of view on the problem, listening skills can be taught.

These illustrations show the flexibility of roleplaying as a training device to improve human relations understanding and skills. The particular case and approach must be tailored to fit the situation with which the trainer is dealing. In any event, there is little reason to doubt the idea that human relations training provides the most challenging and rewarding area for the application of roleplaying.

Executive Training

It was pointed out earlier that special consideration would be given to two specific training areas. The first of these, human relations, has been considered in some detail. Executive training, the second area, presents some unique problems. These problems are not a matter of training theory or practice but rather have to do with the occasional hesitancy of industrial trainers to use roleplaying in executive training programs. A review of recent trends in management education may help to dispel any doubts the reader may have concerning the value of roleplaying as an executive training tool.

Trends in Management Education

"Within the last two decades, under the exigencies of depression and war, management has carried on its own revolution—a revolution of self-improvement."[3] The thousands of executives pouring into the American Management Association's courses for managers, the Advanced Management Course at Harvard and the many other management training centers throughout the country attest to the increasing value placed on executive training and development. Awareness that management is a skilled profession with its own body of knowledge has grown at an increasing tempo in recent years. The problem of defining executive training needs and objectives has attracted the attention of many observers of the management

---

3. Charles E. Redfield, *Communication in management.* Chicago: The University of Chicago Press, 1953.

scene. In 1951, Roethlisberger clarified the educational needs of executives:

What industry and business must have in their supervisory and administrative groups is more educated people . . . not more trained seals. . . . By an "educated person" I mean a person (1) who knows what he does not know; (2) who has an honest perplexity and curiosity about his personal experiences; (3) who has a stop, look, and listen attitude toward his own experience and is capable of re-evaluating and learning from it; and (4) who has some skills in the direction of being able to receive communication from others.[4]

Murray identified executives' needs in this way: "In industry the leader must have perceptiveness, insight, and know-how at a much higher level. He must be much more of a scientist. He must be an artist and a philosopher as well."[5] Appley focused on the intangible needs of the manager when he said: "An enlightened manager is an artist. He is highly skilled in individual effectiveness with people."[6]

These comments are representative of the comparatively recent trend in management education, a trend toward concern with social skills—the ability to relate effectively to other people, to be more aware of one's own behavior and its effect on others.

The era of Taylor and Gilbreth left its stamp on management in the form of a more scientific and systematic approach to problems of administration. Automation, operations research, linear programing, and other scientific techniques are the modern-day counterparts of the original systems and methods work which scientific management practitioners originated.

Almost simultaneously the work of Mayo and Roethlis-

4. F. J. Roethlisberger, "Training supervisors in human relations." *Harvard Business Review*, 1951, 29 (5), 50.

5. Elwood Murray, "How an educator looks at industrial activities in the field of communication." *Journal of Communication*, 1956, 6 (2).

6. Lawrence A. Appley, "An enlightened manager." *The President's Scratch Pad*, 1956, 29 (6), *Management News*.

berger was establishing the foundation for a humanistic movement in industry, which has been the basis for an expanding concern with executives' interpersonal and human relations skills.

A Paradox

This new trend in management thinking and education presents some rather paradoxical problems for the training practitioner. Up until now he has been primarily concerned with selling the need for human relations training and the development of social skills. He now finds that his students are as aware of the need as he is. In fact, in many instances, the executive can speak with authority and erudition about human relations principles and theories. The executive no longer wants to know "What?" or "Why?", he now wants to know "How?". Roleplaying is essentially a "how to" technique. It presents training potentialities which cannot be duplicated by other methods. The greatest single value of roleplaying in executive training can be realized in utilizing it as a "how-to" technique for developing social skills.

Application

The application of roleplaying in executive training programs actually presents very few special problems. The same basic techniques which are used in human relations training are suitable. In fact, the increasing awareness among executives concerning their need for improved social skills often makes roleplaying particularly appealing.

When structured roleplaying cases are used, the content must, of course, be suitable to an executive group. This does not require changing the basic issues involved, merely "dressing" these issues in new clothing. For example, earlier in this chapter a case was used as part of an example of human relations training for foremen. The case involved a manager (foreman) and three subordinates (machine operators). The manager wanted the subordinates to respond to a particular need, i. e. to agree to work overtime to fill a special order. The case was used to increase the participants understanding of human behavior, i. e. behavior is caused.

Here is how the case might appear when adapted for an executive group:

ROLE I

Sam Jones, Executive Vice President: You are the chief operating executive of this company and report directly to the President and Chairman of the Board. About a year ago you recommended that an expansion program that had been underway for several years should be curtailed. The Board, however, voted to continue the program. Yesterday the President called you in and told you that the company must now retrench and that costs must be reduced by 10 per cent. You feel that if the Board had acted on your original suggestion this drastic cut in costs wouldn't be necessary. You know that most of your division executives aren't going to like this move. But it's about time they came back down to earth.

ROLE II

Bill Thompson, V.P. Production: You were recently promoted to your present job and now report to Sam Jones, Executive V.P. You've heard rumblings about a new push to cut costs. You have been getting ready to recommend the purchase of about $25,000 of new equipment. You know the equipment will pay for itself in about 6 years and it has a life of about 12. It would reduce some production headaches and you'd still like to purchase it. Nevertheless, you're new on this job and you don't know your boss too well. It might be better if you gave him a chance to build some confidence in you before arguing about something you can get along without.

ROLE III

Phil Streeter, V.P. Sales: (This role corresponds to ROLE IV *in the foreman training case.)* You have been with this company about 15 years and, under your direction, sales have been increasing steadily.

120

You've been trying for some time to get approval for a special promotional campaign which you're sure would substantially increase sales volume. You talked to the President about it at lunch one day and he seemed to be in favor of the idea. Later you learned that the Exec. V.P. had convinced the President that the campaign was not worth while. The V.P. always seems willing to spend more money on research and development—he's an engineer by profession—but he just has no appreciation of marketing techniques. His unwillingness to spend money on promotion can really hurt the company.

This case has many of the same interpersonal ingredients as the foreman training case. The boss has subordinates who, because of their past experience, will respond differently to the same stimulus. In the foreman case the one machine operator didn't want to work overtime, another was reasonably willing to work. In this case one division manager will resist cutting costs, the other will be reasonably co-operative. In both instances roleplaying can be used to teach a basic human relations principle or as a basis for training in interpersonal skills.

Summary

Roleplaying is applicable in a great many training situations. It is useful in methods training, problem-solving, and increasing personal effectiveness. Basic training approaches can be broken down into three categories:

Method-centered roleplaying is intended to teach specific methods and techniques. Here the emphasis is on procedure rather than on attitudes, feelings, and random forces which may effect the implementation of the procedure.

Problem-centered roleplaying is designed to increase the participant's ability to handle specific problem situations which he faces. Here the focus is on common problems. Rather than dealing with step-by-step methods, the training situation is designed to deal with the task of increasing understanding, and changing attitudes. Although the trainer deals with individual problems, he is primarily concerned with problems from which standards of behavior and performance can be generalized.

Individual-centered roleplaying is used to deal with the individual's personal problems in handling situations which he faces. Here, although common supervisory problems may be dealt with, the focus tends to be on the individual and his own personal blocks and attitudes.

Human relations and executive training are two of the most challenging areas in which roleplaying can be applied. Roleplaying, is most useful as a "how to" training technique. Human relations training is concerned with how to relate and respond to people. Executive training is concerned with how to develop the ability to achieve results through individuals and groups.

Giving Information

GROWING TECHNOLOGY, increased organizational complexity, and the development of new management techniques in industry have brought with them an increased need for information. Technicians and administrators need more data on which to base decisions. Production workers need to be communicated with concerning company-wide programs and policies. Supervisors and managers need more facts about new techniques of management. Changes in methods, procedures, and systems must be communicated. In the modern industrial organization the process of instructing and informing never ceases.

Areas of Application

Roleplaying can be used to inform and instruct in almost every situation in which films, lectures, and demonstrations are suitable. Effective human relations, safety practices, interviewing and, in fact, any skill or principle which involves interaction between people, can be demonstrated through roleplaying. Here are some typical examples:

Safety

An instructor in a safety program wishes to show his students why people frequently resist using safety aids such as goggles, machine guards, safety helmets, etc. Instead of merely talking about typical employee reactions to accident prevention devices, he prepares several group members to act out one or more situations. He may provide them with "skeleton" scripts and let them fill in the dialogue or he may briefly explain their roles to them before the session. At any rate, rather than a lecture about how people behave, a roleplaying enactment can be used to dramatize the situation. The group members observe the enactment in the same way that they would observe any audio-visual presentation. The enactment produces more interest and discussion than a lecture or printed summary of the problem.

Interviewing

A lecturer wishes to explain the nondirective interviewing process to his audience. He finds it hard to get across how to conduct a nondirective interview. He sets up a hypothetical problem and has several assistants act it out. Now, he can continue the lecture with specific references to the interview which his audience has just witnessed.

Labor Relations

An industrial relations director sets up a new procedure for handling employee complaints and grievances. He finds that when he tries to explain the procedure to production foremen he has difficulty in holding their attention. He includes a realistic roleplay of a grievance situation. The roleplay is entertaining and provocative—it raises procedural questions to which the foremen don't know the answers. Now, as the industrial relations man begins to answer these questions he has the attention and interest of his audience.

Applications

The above illustrations serve to show the fundamental value of roleplaying as an information-giving device. The roleplaying enactment is used by the instructor as an audio-visual device. Although the audience remains passive the enactment attracts and focuses attention, stimulates interest and dramatizes an interpersonal situation.

Information-giving roleplaying can be used to build a deeper understanding of a fairly complex problem. A group of field salesmen have been accepting orders which are difficult for the production department to fill. Because of their lack of understanding of the company's production operations, they have permitted customers to order nonstandard items which do not fit established manufacturing specifications. They have promised unrealistic delivery dates.

The salesmen are invited to attend a series of training sessions. The first session opens with a lecture by the production manager briefly reviewing the manufacturing process. Slides are used to illustrate key manufacturing operations. To dramatize a typical problem some of the production people roleplay the handling of a sales order. The salesmen witness the demonstration but do not take part. They see the manufacturing superintendent approach a foreman and tell him an order has just been received for one thousand units of product X. The field salesman in the roleplay has accepted minor changes in specifications for the product and has promised delivery in two weeks. The audience hears the foreman will tell the superintendent that the specification changes will require retooling of a substantial part of his equipment. This will result in a great deal of machine "down time." To meet the delivery date it will be necessary for many of the production workers to work overtime. The foreman points out that he will have to hold up another order if the superintendent wants him to get this one out on time. The salesmen see the two production people struggling with problems of scheduling, machine "down time," overtime costs and the effect of the production specification change on the morale of the work force. They see, too, that another order must be held up to meet the special requirements of this one.

In this application, a lecture, visual aids and a roleplaying demonstration have been used with the same basic purpose. *The goal of the session is to increase the salesmen's understanding and knowledge of problems created by their behavior. The ultimate objective is to produce changes in the way the salesmen handle orders in the field.*

Roleplaying makes it possible for salesmen to see how production supervisors dealt with problems created in the field. The discussion between the foreman and superintendent has more impact on the audience than pages of facts and figures documenting the cost of handling special sales orders.

These examples show roleplaying for information-giving as a device to focus attention, stimulate interest, and increase understanding. Applications can be broken down more specifically into three categories:

1. To increase general understanding and knowledge.
2. To teach specific methods.
3. To prepare for training.

Increasing General Understanding

The purpose of information-giving and instruction is to change behavior. When information is communicated concerning "principles of human relations" or "safety practices" the goal is to improve the way in which group members handle human relations or safety problems back on the job. There are situations, however, in which the goal of information-giving is less specific. For example, a company may wish to have its employees increase their understanding of how collective bargaining works. The employees may be invited to attend a "mock" negotiations session, i. e. members of the union and management act out a hypothetical collective bargaining situation. The general goal of this session is to increase the employees' sense of involvement in management-union relations and to help improve communications between union members supervisors, but in the final analysis no specific behavioral change is anticipated. Nevertheless, some generalized improvement in the way in which employees react and respond to union-management problems may be expected.

Teaching Specific Methods

There are many situations in which management must require employees to conform to some established policy or legal requirement. For example, bank tellers must be instructed in basic procedures relative to check cashing, deposits, withdrawals, etc. A roleplaying enactment may be used to show the new teller how he must behave in conducting banking transactions. In effect, the enactment is intended to communicate what must be done.

Preparing for Training

Finally, information-giving or instructional roleplaying may be used to prepare a group for action training. The use of a

127

new form for guiding the supervisor in reviewing his subordinate's performance may be *demonstrated* through roleplaying. The demonstration does not directly change the behavior or actions of the observer-trainees but does prepare them to participate in action-learning situations which will, hopefully, result in more effective behavior.

There are a great many situations in which basic understanding must precede the development of skills and techniques. The communication of principles, theories, and proven methods can often be made more effective through roleplaying. For example, in many sales training programs instruction in basic principles of salesmanship often precedes actual training in sales interviewing skills. In such cases roleplaying has the advantage of increasing the impact of rather dry material by dramatizing it.

Summary

In any situation where the goal is to demonstrate, emphasize, or clarify a principle, method, or complex set of facts involving interaction between people, roleplaying is useful. Roleplayers may be provided with scripts or may be extensively instructed in their role assignment. (In some situations where briefing or advance preparation of roles is not possible, the roleplayers may be given a brief oral description of a situation and asked to act it out spontaneously.)

The actors in a roleplaying demonstration are serving as living audio-visual aids. They act out the scene based on what the instructor has told them to do. Unlike roleplayers in a training or testing situation, participants in an information-giving session are not expected to use their own judgment in what they say or do because they are limited by the instructions. Nor is the audience expected to move into action. Their role is to look and listen, to learn through observation.

Roleplaying to communicate information can often succeed in attracting attention, stimulating interest, and provoking discussion in situations which more didactic approaches are ineffective.

Finally, and most significantly, demonstration roleplaying can produce a deeper understanding of the problem under discussion. It has the advantage of simulating real situations and providing a greater degree of audience involvement.

Testing

ALL HUMAN BEHAVIOR can be considered as the testing of hypotheses. If I come to a puddle and jump over it I am testing the hypothesis that I have judged the size of the puddle correctly and have evaluated my jumping capacity adequately. I may slip just before I jump—this means I didn't evaluate the surface properly, or if I do not clear the obstacle, this means I didn't judge myself and conditions well. A person who consistently does not evaluate himself and his surroundings accurately will probably not survive long in an environment which has many hazards, which is one reason we institutionalize the insane and the feebleminded.

In industry, there are many judgments required for success. The worker has to know how to size up his fellows and supervisors. Those in supervisory positions have to understand their subordinates, peers and superiors.

In the selection of personnel, whether it be a girl to act as receptionist, or the upgrading of an hourly worker to foreman, or the appointment of a president, someone has to make decisions. These decisions can be crucial for the success of an organization. It is evident that if one hires a dishonest treasurer he could readily destroy the organization. A president who consistently makes poor decisions can ruin a company. That human errors contribute to the rise and fall of organizations can hardly be doubted.

But what can one do in situations that call for judgment when there is almost no basis for adequate decisions? Here are two salesmen who are applying for the same job, and they have almost identical backgrounds. One may be a potential crackerjack, the other a dud. How can one tell? Ordinarily, we can set as a general rule: keeping the judgment capacity of selectors as a constant, the *more* information we have, the better the decision. And then we can add the very important qualification, the more *pertinent* the information the better.

The sources of information we use are diverse: we can get historical data, interview data, test data, and observational data. Offhand, all are valuable, but for those decisions that have to do with human relations skills, such as supervising, the best kind of information is observation. That is, if you can actually see how the person does in various situations, this is more important than hearsay evidence (testimonials, letters of recommendations), or secondary evidence (tests, interviews, and impressions).

Let us consider the use of psychological tests. Tests can be divided into two general types, standardized and projective.

Standardized Tests

A standardized test is given in an invarying manner. Its procedures are rigorously established by the test constructor and the examiner has to use the test like a laboratory instrument in the exact procedure specified in the manual. The subject is restricted and can only do specific things to get a good score. After the test is over, it is scored mechanically and raw scores are transmuted to interpretable sources such as percentiles and ratings.

If a person gets a rating of A on the Strong Interest Test for the salesman variable, this is interpreted to mean that this subject's interests are similar to those of salesmen and thus he may be a good bet as a salesman. If a child gets an IQ of 125 on the Stanford Binet Test, this means he displayed superior intelligence on that instrument and that he may be exepected to do well in scholastic work.

A standardized test is not only standardized in terms of administration and scoring; it is also standardized in terms of interpretations. If the test is suitably administered to people to whom it is applicable, then the final product—the score—is rigorously interpreted.

Projective Tests

A projective test is very different from the standardized test in that the examiner is all-important. He does not follow specific instructions and is not limited to single dimensions of interpretations. Both the subject and the examiner have much more freedom.

For example, the Rorschach test, the best-known and the most-studied of the projective tests, consists of ink blots, to which subjects are to respond in terms of what they see. Instead of being asked to answer A-B-C-D, or writing letters or numbers, they now can respond with anything whatsoever.

The examiner listens to the responses, records them, and later analyzes them, and on the basis of his judgment of the meaning of the responses, considering up to one hundred different variables such as the location of the perception, how it was seen, its content, the reaction times, the approach to the cards, and so forth, he may come to a variety of conclusions about the individual with respect to personality factors including such items as drive, intelligence, types of interests, nature of personal problems, psychiatric diagnoses, etc. While almost all examiners will more or less come to the same conclusions using standardized tests, there will be considerably more variation in using projective techniques.

Roleplaying like the Rorschach is a projective technique. Different observers may see different things and may interpret them in different ways. The subject, as in the case of the Rorschach, can vary his responses to the stimuli made by the antagonists, and what he says and how he says it, gives observers insights into how he reacts to life, what kind of a person he is, and what may possibly be wrong with his behavior—generally and specifically.

Theory of Roleplaying for Testing

The validity of a test depends on the agreement between the interpretation of the test and the reality which it is supposed to measure. If, let us say, someone creates a new test and calls it a test of intelligence, in order to validate it, he has to prove that it really does measure intelligence, which he can do in a number of ways. For example, he may correlate his test with other tests of intelligence; or he may check scores of children of varying ages; or he may use the test in a clinical fashion, seeing if his predictions work out for individuals.

The validity of roleplaying as a test depends on the degree of reality measurement that takes place: does the individual in performing "on the stage" bear any resemblance to the individual in real life? Is the artificial situation and the contrived problem such to elicit behavior typical of the individual? This is a crucial question, and we have some evidence to the effect that roleplaying is a rather good procedure for understanding others. Let us consider the evidence.

Clinical Judgments

Roleplaying has been used by many psychologists who know their patients rather well, and who have found in the playing of roles, people tend to become themselves, and due to the stresses of having to deal with antagonists rapidly, they are unable to act in any way but their usual manner. We obtain the same type of evidence from subjects, especially after exciting sessions where there is a good deal of give and take, that the situation seemed very realistic. We not infrequently find that people get excited and emotional on the stage and seem completely natural in their reactions.

Experimental Evidence

Borgatta (16) conducted a classical experiment to investigate the relationship between actual natural behavior, roleplaying behavior, and test results. He found real behavior could be better predicted from roleplaying than from psychological tests.

Logical Evidence

It would seem on the basis of theory that a function is the best measure of itself. That is to say if we wish to know if a girl can typewrite, the best way is to get her to type, rather than to try to determine this by an interview; school ratings, or other processes. So, too, if we say that we are interested in determining what a person's natural behavior is in complex situations where he has to be in interaction with other people, it seems evident that a test of exactly that type is the best.

All of us are always "testing" other people. That is to say we observe them and we make inferences from our observations. We see a shabby person weaving on the street and conclude that he is drunk. In most cases our judgment is correct, even though infrequently the weaving may be due to other causes. We see a very well-dressed elderly gentleman walking down the street and are convinced he must be a respectable and wealthy person—although he may have just gotten out of prison and may be on the way to ask someone for a loan. When we are introduced to people we make judgments about them from how they look, how they act, and how they talk. The snap impressions that we make about others, although they may be wrong in some cases, probably have a good deal of general validity to them.

The interview is an example of a projective test. A person enters the office, looking, let us say, for a job. A job is open and we have some concept in our mind of the kind of person we want in terms of personality, character, and ability. A good interviewer will be able to size up the individual rapidly, coming to his conclusions on the basis of the many impressions he gets of the individual. Research on interviews indicates that people come to have rather definite impressions of others on the basis of very little information.

In considering methods for the evaluation of people, there are at least four considerations to keep in mind: (a) the purpose of the evaluation, (b) who is being evaluated, (c) who is evaluating, and (d) necessary validity. Here are some examples:

1. A child of six is brought to a school and the principal wants to determine whether the child is ready for the first grade.

Probably the best procedure here is to call in a school psychologist who will give the child reading readiness and scholastic achievement tests.

2. An employer wishes to know whether an applicant is really a competent truck driver.

Here he may ask the applicant to get into a truck and show how he can run it.

3. A young man applies for a position as a junior executive. He is just out of college and has no work experience.

In this case, roleplaying seems to be the preferred way of testing.

Now, none of these procedures may be really good. The child may be disturbed by the experience and do poorly. The truck driver may have skill but may be unreliable. The junior executive may do poorly on a roleplaying test but really be a good potential bet. No test is perfect. But everything considered, the best test of a function is the function itself. And to the degree that the procedures are realistic, to that extent they are valid.

We can take an example from a simple procedure such as running. Ordinarily a runner will run a distance very closely to a specific time. A miler who can do the distance in 4:10 one day is very likely to do it within one or two seconds of that time the next day; but somedays people vary from their usual abilities, and will either exceed their usual performances or fall short.

Roleplaying is the theoretically preferred procedure for the evaluation of complex interactive abilities—where the individuals have to think on their feet and deal with one or several others—where emotional, intellectual and behavioral elements occur simultaneously or in close succession. To test elements separately and then attempt to synthesize them is dangerous; a person is not merely the sum of his parts—there is more to him than that.

We may approach this subject from a different angle. Let

us say that an individual is interviewed for a particular job, and is told that he is not satisfactory. Suppose that he is convinced he can do the job, and that those who are judging him are wrong in their opinions. He may have all kinds of arguments about his training, willingness, and experience. What would be his final argument? Simply this: "Give me a chance." Now, the logic is unimpeachable. Surely the best way to know whether any person will succeed is to try him out. How can one really know in advance? The answer is that one cannot know. One can only guess on the basis of the best evidence available.

But if roleplaying is a test of itself: that is to say if a person plays the role on the stage that he plays in real life, then roleplaying is a method of giving somebody a chance of trying out. The question becomes once again: what is the purpose of roleplaying for testing? Its purpose is to see how people interact with others in specific situations. Just as it makes sense to evaluate a person who wants to sing by testing him for singing, so too it makes sense to evaluate a person who is applying for a job that concerns dealing with others to test him by a means that involves dealing with others.

In short, roleplaying for testing is a tryout procedure, putting an individual in a realistic situation where he operates holistically and dynamically. In a short space of time observers can come to conclusions about individuals' abilities.

Purposes of Testing

Roleplaying used for testing has two general purposes: *evaluation* and *analysis*. Actually, both are variations of the same general purpose: understanding. However, it may be well to understand the purposes generally and in terms of examples.

Evaluation

Evaluation means classification. After an individual is tested, he is given a label. Usually the labels are part of a series that cover the entire spectrum of valuation. For example, there may be dichotomous labeling such as "acceptable—not-acceptable," or there may be labels such as "A-B-C-D" with various connotations. We may compare evaluations to military physical examinations, which are strictly concerned with grading people into physical classes of fitness.

Analysis

Analysis means the evaluation of subparts, the comparative ratings of parts, the comprehension of the meaning of isolated elements. Analysis in roleplaying is usually done for the purpose of understanding strong and weak points of an individual or as a process to eliminate weak parts and strengthen good parts.

Impersonal Purposes

Up to this point stress has been placed on roleplaying in terms of individuals. Roleplaying can be done for quite a different purpose: to evaluate procedures, regardless of individuals. For example: a sales presentation can be analyzed and evaluated through roleplaying.

Examples

Let us now put some flesh on the theoretical bones we have assembled by giving illustrations of roleplaying used for evaluation and analysis. One should keep in mind that many of the exciting possiblities of roleplaying are largely unexplored and have not been used in industry to the extent that they have been in military and other areas.

Evaluation

The president of a small firm selling restaurant products, had considerable difficulty in finding suitable salesmen for his business. Interviewing, checking references, training the salesmen, having them go with more experienced salesmen was expensive—and the rate of attrition due to resignations or unsatisfactory performance was too high. It was his experience that only one good salesman was found out of every seven hired —and only one was hired out of every seven interviewed.

Roleplaying was offered as a solution—and the procedure worked as follows: all candidates were invited to a hotel conference room, where the president explained the difficulty he had, and how unnecessary it seemed to him to hire people who just did not work out. In place of asking salesmen to fill questionnaires, checking their references, interviewing them, asking them to be tried out, he told them he would prefer to test them. Each person was to enter the testing room, carrying a suitcase of samples. Each salesman was to read a sheet containing a description of the product. In the testing room he was to make, successively, three presentations to three different people.

In the testing room, three of the veteran salesmen served as antagonists. One handled the salesman in a friendly manner, another in a rough manner, and the third in a hesitating manner. Each was told to purchase material if he felt like it. The antagonists came in, one at a time, and did not see or hear the other presentations. After each presentation, the antagonist wrote his judgment of the salesmen; and so did the observers consisting of the president, three of his salesmen and a psychologist.

Ten salesmen were tested in the morning and ten more in the afternoon. This procedure was repeated one day a month for four months. The batting average of one success out of seven increased to one out of three. The president of the firm, calculating expenses alone, felt his costs had dropped one-half while success in selection had improved over one hundred per cent.

The reason for the value of this procedure was simply that the applicants were tested "at work" in different situations by the judgment of a number of experts who could see how the salesmen conducted themselves with different, but typical restaurant owners and managers. They were, in a sense, "tried out" in realistic situations.

From the point of view of the applicants, less time was wasted in being evaluated—and they got a meal out of it as well as some insights into their performances.

Another use of roleplaying for evaluation illustrates how this procedure can be used in real life situations without special equipment or special assistants during the daily course of work.

The position of receptionist was opened in a large office and an announcement was made to the other girls already working that they could apply for this job which had higher prestige and slightly higher salary than typing and clerking positions. All applicants were generally familiar with the work of the receptionist. At the end of work one day, the personnel man took the applicants one at a time, asked them to sit behind the receptionist's desk and he then played the role of a number of people who might come to the receptionist with a number of queries and for a number of purposes. Each girl was independently "tested" by the personnel man, and he served not only as the director, but as the antagonist and the observer.

Somewhat to his surprise he found that one girl, whom he would never have considered for the job since she had appeared somewhat mousy and also had been in the office a relatively short time, did the most outstanding job of playing the role of receptionist, showing wit, sparkle, and aplomb. She was hired and was found to be entirely satisfactory when she played the role eight hours a day.

Analysis

In considering roleplaying for analysis we enter a more complex area, since we are now no longer dealing with a simple over-all decision but rather with the examination and evaluation of many elements seen in dynamic functioning. Some cases in evidence of the use of roleplaying for analysis may help explain the procedure.

An engineer had been made the works manager of a firm, supplanting a retired employee who had been considered outstandingly successful. The engineer had more than seven years of experience in the firm, was well trained, was considered a hard worker, was respected by his fellow engineers for his technical competence and was regarded as a "comer." However, he turned out to be a complete failure in his new position. He seemed to antagonize everyone. Turnover rates of personnel went up, production dropped, and morale was visibly reduced. Despite the fact that he was regarded as an outstanding engineer, he seemed to be a very poor administrator, although no one quite knew what was wrong with him. At the insistence of his own supervisor—the president of the firm, he enrolled in a course designed to develop leaders.

He played a number of typical situations before observers, other supervisors who kept notes and then explained to him in detail what he did they thought was wrong. Entirely concerned with efficiency, he was merciless in criticizing people who made mistakes, condemning them to too great an extent. He did not really listen to others, had little interest in their ideas, and wanted to have his own way—which was the only right way. The entire group of managers explained, in great detail, a number of human relations errors that he made.

One by one, these errors were discussed and one by one he rejected accepting them as errors. He admitted his behavior, and defended it. He refused to change his approach, and instead he attacked high and low—the officials for their not backing him, and subordinates for their laxness, stupidity, and stubbornness. After the diagnosing, he left the course, convinced that it could do him no good.

We may say that his problem was diagnosed but that he refused treatment. The engineer turned works manager had a particular view of life—and refused to change it. We may say that his attitude was foolish, since he may have been a success had he learned some human relations skills; or we may say that his attitude was commendable, showing his independence of mind, in his refusal to adjust to the opinions of others. In any case, he refused to accept the implications of the analysis, that he needed to be made over.

Another case may be given in illustration of a successful use of analysis, and also of the employment of a procedure for intensive analysis. In a course for supermarket operators, a district manager who had been recently appointed to his position after being outstandingly successful as a store manager, found that in supervising other managers he was having a difficult time. On playing some typical situations before a jury of his peers he showed some characteristics rated as unsatisfactory. He was told he displayed, for example, a sense of superiority—and he answered: "Well, I am supposed to know all the answers, aren't I?" He was criticized for his curtness and abruptness—and he answered: "I am not working to become popular." On being criticized for his arbitrary behavior —he answered: "I have to make decisions. That's my job." In short, as frequently happens in analyses, the individual feels threatened and defends himself. However, in this case the district manager was led to see the errors of his ways. The necessary step between diagnosis and training is acceptance of the validity of the criticisms. How this was accomplished may be described, since this sometimes is a crucial problem.

The director helped tailor-make a check list of the district manager's errors by asking various observers to write out sentences commenting on the mistakes they felt he made. These errors were then collected and written on a blackboard, condensing similar ideas. Eighteen errors were located, and then the director asked each individual to vote whether or not they felt that this manager had made the particular errors. They were asked to vote "true" if they thought they had seen him make the error, "false" if they thought he had not; and "cannot say" if they were not certain.

The manager sat behind the group so he could see and count the hands that went up, and the director wrote the numbers on the blackboard. No comments were made during the voting. The results looked as follows:

Errors made by John Jewel
(Judges = 40)

	True	False	Cannot Say
1. Too bossy; arbitrary	35	2	3
2. Too loud; forceful	34	3	3
3. Does not listen	27	8	5
4. Interrupts too much	25	8	7
5. Not willing to compromise	25	9	6
6. Too aggressive	25	3	13
7. Not friendly	21	10	7
8. Too abrupt	20	15	5
9. Talks too much	18	5	13
10. Insulting	16	3	21
11. Bad language used	15	0	25
12. Not co-operative	11	13	16
13. Not sympathetic	9	19	12
14. Does not understand person	6	23	11
15. Does not understand situation	5	25	10
16. Disinterested in people	4	10	26
17. Hostile attitude	3	10	27
18. Cruel	2	30	8

The first eight of these eighteen statements, which received at least one-half of the votes, were duplicated to form an analysis checklist for the particular manager, and when this particular manager roleplayed in other situations, the members checked any items that appeared. To prevent the manager from deliberately controlling himself only during the sessions, they were rather lengthy (about twenty minutes), the situations were imperfectly described to the manager so that he would not know what to expect, new antagonists were brought on the scene unexpectedly, and the antagonists were instructed to deliberately behave in such ways as to upset the manager and get him to operate in a manner for which he had been previously criticized.

After every session, the check marks were totaled up and graphed, and in this way the supervisor's progress was charted.

Summary

In life we learn to play our roles and we "freeze" into patterns which become so habitual that we are not really aware of what we do. We can see others more clearly than we can see ourselves, and others can see us better than we see ourselves. To learn what we do is the first step for improvement. To accept the validity of the judgments of others is the second step. To want to change is the third step. To practice new procedures under guided supervision and with constant feedback is the fourth step. To use these new ways in daily life is the last step. Roleplaying used for analysis follows these general steps leading to training.

When an evaluative situation is set up, and no concern is with the details that lead to an over-all estimate, we say that roleplaying is used for evaluation. Observers can see a person engaged in spontaneous behavior, and watch him operating in a totalistic fashion. This behavior is more "veridical"—or true than other testing behavior for some types of evaluation, and so can give quick and accurate estimates of complex functioning.

While roleplaying for testing is not too well understood at the present time, it represents one of the major uses of this procedure.

Spontaneity Training

THE OBJECTIVE OF THIS CHAPTER is to clarify the distinctions between spontaneity theory and other training concepts. In addition, the basic approach utilized in applying roleplaying will be reviewed. The goal will be to provide the reader with an integrated rationale to aid him in applying roleplaying techniques in this unique training area. The reasons for extracting this particular roleplaying application from the previous discussion of training are twofold:

1. Spontaneity training theory is unique and relatively new.

2. The basic approach used in applying roleplaying to spontaneity training is quite different from those used in other training areas.

As a preface to a consideration of spontaneity training applications and approaches, a brief discussion and review of learning theory in general, and roleplaying theory, in particular, is necessary.

Learning Theory

Without probing deeply into classical learning theory, it can be said that the learning process usually contains one or more of the following ingredients; trial and error, practice, imitation, and guidance.

Whether one is involved in learning a basic motor skill or a complicated social response, one or more of these ingredients is present. In learning to play golf the beginner typically receives some basic instruction. He tries out what he has learned and corrects his mistakes as he goes along. He watches more experienced players and attempts to imitate their swing. Above all, he practices. Roleplaying provides opportunity for capitalizing on all of these activities. The participant can practice, correct his own mistakes, imitate others, and receive guidance from "experts."

The belief, shared by many practitioners, that the integration of these various ingredients of learning provides the necessary rationale for roleplaying is incomplete according to spontaneity theory. The essence of spontaneity roleplaying theory lies in still another direction. This is not to say that trial and error, imitation, guidance, and practice are not significant considerations in applying the technique. However, there is a more pervasive consideration basic to spontaneity roleplaying theory.

Spontaneity Learning Theory

Some indications of a more complete and sophisticated rationale for roleplaying may be gleaned from the comments of contemporary practitioners in the training field. Katz, for example, points out:

The first intention (of training) is to help participants increase their awareness of the adequacies and inadequacies of their observations and actions in situations involving people. Until a man recognizes the need to improve, he will not exert much effort in improving himself.[1]

Argyris points up a frequently overlooked aspect of learning when he says:

> Although a man may be taught *about* self-insight and human skills of living, these can be acquired only through living in and learning from a stream of life events we call experience. Experience, per se, never teaches anyone anything, the operative factor is the use the individual makes of it.[2]

Bradford (17) summarized the conditions necessary to bring about changes in behavior as follows:

1. Exposure of behavior
2. Feedback of effectiveness
3. Climate encouraging change
4. Necessary information appropriately timed
5. Opportunities for experimentation and practice
6. Opportunities to explore problems of application

Lewin's theory of change involving the "unfreezing" of "frozen" behavior was reviewed earlier. (See page 31) The significance of feedback in the learning process was also stressed. (See page 74)

Roleplaying, applied in the training area, can meet all these conditions. Participants have an opportunity to increase "their awareness of the adequacies and inadequacies of their observations and actions." (17) There is ample opportunity for learning from "the stream of life events we call experience." (17) With proper direction all of the conditions which Brad-

---

1. Robert L. Katz, "Human relations skills can be sharpened." *Harvard Business Review*, 1956, 34 (4), 61-72.

2. Chris Argyris, "Executive development programs: some unresolved problems." *Personnel*, 1956, 33, 33-41.

ford has outlined can be met. Opportunities for feedback and experimentation with new approaches are present. Thus, conceptually, roleplaying meets the test of suitability both from the point of view of classical learning theory and contemporary thinking. However, the origin of contemporary roleplaying lies neither in classical learning theory nor in the thinking outlined above.

Spontaneity Theory

Moreno has defined spontaneity as: "An adequate response to a new situation or a new and adequate response to an old situation."[3] One implication of this definition is that the trainer is not teaching the *individual to conform to some* predetermined standard or norm, rather he is attempting to create a spontaneous climate in which new approaches, new methods, and new responses are born, or in which old responses are suitably fitted into new situations. Spontaneity means the ability to respond to forces present in a given situation, without being constricted and inhibited by rigid patterns of behavior. From a practical point of view the ability to respond adequately to new situations requires both an awareness of what is going on in the situation and the ability to react adequately to what is going on. At first blush these ideas seem to fit in quite well with the point of view that behavior must be exposed, that there must be feedback, and that the operational factor is experience. It seems that Moreno is saying the same thing that everyone else is saying, but in a slightly different way. However, spontaneity theory introduces a new dimension to learning theory.

3. J. L. Moreno, *Who shall survive?* Beacon, N. Y.: Beacon Press, 1953.

Another Dimension of Learning

In the genesis of learning there was a time when the possibilities for imitation, guidance, and feedback were minimal. Practicing and learning by experience must have been preceded by the creation of the thing to be practiced or learned. Thus, original learning consisted of responding to an unknown environment. However, man brought something indigenous to the learning situation. He brought his own creativity and spontaneity.

Perhaps this idea can be clarified through an analogy:

We now take it for granted that a child learns the language of his time and place through guidance, imitation, feedback, and the additional ingredients and considerations previously outlined. But what of the origin of language? For some one, at some time it must have been almost a purely creative and spontaneous act. One can imagine man's first discovery that he could produce and alter sounds. There was no one to imitate and no one to "analyze his performance." There were certainly no standards of behavior to adhere to. The fact that there are in the neighborhood of three thousand separate and distinct languages indicates the many avenues open to him in developing language. One can imagine that he began to "play" with sound before he formulated it into language. One can find verification of this idea by observing the behavior of infants as they discover language. Their use of sound is uninhibited and uncontrolled. They seem to be making sounds for the sheer joy of creating something of their own. They produce sounds that they have never heard before, many of which will ultimately be discarded.

One can argue that the sheer production of sound with no manifest results, and no interaction is merely random behavior. On the other hand, one can take the point of view that this is the beginning of learning and that guidance, imitation, and analysis are refinements of the process which bring the learning experience into clearer focus. Thus the learning of language begins with action. Moreno summed up this point of view when he said:

> The baby languages are spontaneous language formations of an autistic character. Although they differ from the organized language of the adult, they have a structure of their own which is more actional than verbal, closer to the spontaneous act than to the frozen word.[4]

The implications of the language analogy suggests two ideas basic to spontaneity theory: (1) The individual brings something of his own to the learning situation. He brings creative and spontaneous forces within himself which he may tap to meet the needs of the situation in which he finds himself and ultimately shape to conform his behavior to the standards of the society of which he is a member. (2) The sheer act of creating and experimenting with new responses precedes the shaping of these responses to fit predetermined standards of behavior, and in fact precedes the establishment of the standards themselves.

Action vs. Analysis

It now becomes apparent that there are two quite different ways of approaching training. One approach is essentially analytical. Its objective is to increase the individual's understanding of the separate elements of his performance or behavior which have an impact on his total effectiveness.

The second approach depends upon action to produce results. Its objective is to increase the participant's awareness of the range of responses available to him. This goal is not

---

4. Moreno, *op. cit.* p. 33.

accomplished through analyzing his behavior but rather by creating conditions which make it possible for the trainee to discover and utilize his own potentialities.

The relationship of training applications, objectives, and methods can now be further clarified. The objective of training is to improve performance and change behavior by using methods which produce involvement and learning by doing. One approach to implementing this goal is to establish conditions which provide for effective and acceptable feedback concerning the participant's behavior. These conditions make it possible for analytical comments and interpretation of behavior by others to be communicated with more impact and effect. This approach depends upon analysis for success.

The second approach involves providing conditions which make it possible for the participant to become more spontaneous. In this approach the participant is encouraged to widen his range of responses and to experiment with new techniques, new methods, and new feelings. Analysis, in the usual sense, is minimal and the emphasis is on action. The relationship between objectives, applications, and methods in the training area is schematically shown below:

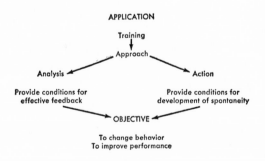

In the previous chapter method-centered, problem-centered, and individual-centered roleplaying were discussed. The emphasis in these discussions was on analytical techniques, e.g. a trainee demonstrates how he would instruct a new employee and group members make suggestions as to how he could have been more effective. They *analyze* his performance and *feedback* the results of their analysis. The process of exposing behavior, analyzing actions, and feeding back suggestions for improvement can be used in all three of the training situations previously described (method-centered, problem-centered, and individual-centered).

However, in sessions where the goal is: (1) to increase the participant's ability to handle complex and changing situations (problem-centered), or (2) to increase the individual's self-awareness and personal effectiveness (individual-centered), an action training approach is frequently useful. Thus, as the above diagram illustrates, both analytical and action approaches can be used to change behavior and improve performance.

The difference between these approaches can be illustrated by a simple illustration:

Two group members are engaged in roleplaying a performance interview. One is playing the part of the supervisor, the other the subordinate. A fairly common occurrence in this kind of roleplay is that the interviewer overparticipates. He does not give his subordinate a chance to talk and to express his feelings and opinions. In an analytical session the effect of the supervisor's behavior can be analyzed and suggestions for more effective ways of dealing with the situation can be solicited from the group. If the session is well directed, the group will have been warmed-up to a common problem and members will be ready for work. A climate will have been established whereby helpful and constructive ideas are not met with defensiveness and rationalization. The trainer has a variety of approaches available to him to feedback to the participant interviewer the effect his behavior may be having on his subordinate:

1. He can stop the action and ask the group for comments. In a brief guided discussion he can be reasonably sure that some member of the group will comment on the supervisor's overparticipation. The trainer can encourage a discussion of the effect of this behavior on the interviewee. He can set up situations which make it possible for the trainees to experiment with better methods.

2. The trainer may, rather than interviewing group members, interview the subordinate. He may say to the subordinate: "Your boss has been talking to you about this problem for some time, how do you feel?" A brief but skillful interview of the subordinate will, in most cases, bring to light some dissatisfaction and negative feeling on his part regarding the supervisor's domination of the interview.

3. An additional alternative for the trainer is to supply group members with observation sheets, which ask specific questions regarding techniques and methods. One of the questions on the sheet might well be: Do you think the subordinate has had sufficient opportunity to express his ideas? The roleplaying enactment can then be permitted to run its course. Subsequently a discussion of the observation sheets and various individual's reactions to the enactment can be solicited.

4. Another alternative is for the trainer to conduct the session along the lines of Lewin's theory of "freeze—unfreeze—refreeze." As ineffective techniques are identified, the trainer can guide the group in unfreezing established attitudes and patterns of behavior which have resulted in ineffective action. Alternate courses of action can be discussed, considered, and finally experimented with through roleplaying. The group can

154

be guided in a discussion which leads toward "freezing" on more effective approaches.

Regardless of the specific techniques used the basic pattern in these sessions includes analyzing the effectiveness of the behavior and methods of various individuals, maximizing feedback between and among participants, and developing more effective ways of handling the situation.

Using this same basic situation as an example, action approaches for dealing with this training problem can now be examined:

In action training where the objective is to provide conditions which lead toward increased spontaneity on the part of the group members, the trainer proceeds in a somewhat different manner. He approaches the session with no preconceived opinions as to how individuals should handle the interviewing situation. He is primarily concerned with producing as much involvement and action as he can. The participant is provided with an opportunity to become aware of or feel the various pressures and forces operative in the interviewing situation. A climate of experimentation is created and concern with "what's right" or "what's wrong" is minimized. As the interview begins and the problem of overparticipation by the supervisor emerges, the trainer discourages analysis and interpretation of this behavior. He attempts to produce more involvement on the part of the roleplayers. Thus, at a given point in the interview, he may ask the players to reverse roles. As a result of this role reversal the supervisor, now in the role of the subordinate, may become more aware of the fact that he was overcontrolling the interview. As he now sits in the subordinate's chair he sees in the supervisor a kind of mirror of himself. As a result he may develop some insight into the effect of his behavior on others. However, this is not the primary goal of the session. Rather the trainer is interested in getting the supervisor involved in as many dimensions of the human interaction as possible. He may introduce a double who sits behind the supervisor (now in the subordinate's role) and expresses some of the feelings that the subordinates have in performance review sessions. Here again further understanding and insight may be developed but no judgments are made as to what is right or wrong and no analysis is permitted. Rather the trainer continues warming-up the roleplayers to the total situation. As the supervisor begins to reverse roles and hears the reactions of doubles he finds himself forgetting that he is in a roleplaying situation. He begins to react to the pressures that are present at the moment. He finds it increasingly difficult to meet the needs of the situation with stereotyped and rigid responses. Gradually he finds himself reacting on the basis of his immediate feelings and using responses which seem most suitable for the situation at hand. As the action increases and he becomes more emotionally involved, he begins creatively and spontaneously to discover new ways of responding.

A natural and justifiable question arises at this point. If in an action-oriented session a participant's behavior cannot be analyzed and interpreted, how does he learn? The answer is that he learns primarily by self-discovery. He has a better chance to learn if his responses are not inhibited by interpretive, analytical comments which stifle the possibilities for experimentation. A further example may help to clarify this idea:

One common objective of sales training programs is to increase the participant's persuasiveness in dealing with customers. In a session where the orientation is primarily analytical a typical comment which often arises after members have observed a sales interview is: "You would be more effective in handling sales interviews if you would smile more." Let us assume that the ideal conditions for an analytical session have been met. The group has been warmed-up to the problem of becoming more persuasive and the individual participant is eager to learn better ways of dealing with his customers. His resistance to the idea that he should smile more is minimal. He listens with great interest and a high degree of motivation. Group members point out to him that persuasiveness and a beaming countenance go hand-in-hand. He welcomes the opportunity to be helped and guided by his associates. And so a helpful group member has commented: "You should smile more." However, what does the analyst really mean by his remark? Does he mean the trainee should smile all the time? Hardly! He means the man should smile at appropriate times. Presumably the matter of degree is also involved—sometimes the man should grin and sometimes he should laugh. Then there is the matter of individual differences—for some men to smile during a sales interview might seem entirely natural, while for others it might be extremely distracting to the customer.

There has been a sincere attempt to help a participant objectify an element of behavior which is essentially subjective. Perhaps through the power of positive thinking and a will to succeed, the individual trainee may learn to turn on a somewhat mechanical and insincere smile at reasonably appropriate times. But such learning is rather superficial and may have little effect on the man's performance on the job. Analysis which is an effective form of information-giving suffers from some of the same limitations associated with didactic methodology.

On the other hand, in an action oriented session where the goal is to produce spontaneity, a smile may appear as one of a number of responses produced as a result of the participant's involvement in various dimensions of the interviewing situation. As he is warmed-up to the sales interviewing enactment and becomes more sensitive to what is going on and more capable of responding to it, he may feel like smiling. The act (smile) is in response to the situation rather than at the direction of an observer. The effect of the act is felt as a part of a process of interaction, for the "customer" reacts to the salesman's behavior. It should be clearly understood, however, that the smile did not occur purely by chance. In spontaneity training, action techniques, such as role reversal and doubling, are utilized to aid the participant in discovering adequate responses. In addition, other forces help the trainer to produce impactful learning experiences. These forces can best be explained by reviewing two often overlooked concepts.

The Actor-Observer Concept

As Argyris (8) points out, people do not necessarily learn from experience. It is not enough to merely act in a situation. Roleplaying, in order to be effective, must produce a successful marriage of the acting and observing function. A person's ability to respond more adequately to the situation in which he finds himself is somewhat dependent upon his ability to become more skillful in observing the effect of his behavior on others. In spontaneity training the possibilities for increasing the individual's effectiveness as both an actor and an observer are maximized. For although the trainee may become deeply involved in acting out a situation, he is nevertheless aware that an audience is present. A few moments before the enactment began he was a part of that audience. In a group where the warmup has been effectively conducted, the player moves into action not only as an individual but as a representative of the group. Psychologically a part of him remains in the group. Coupled with his identification with the audience is the effect of role reversal, doubling, and soliloquy on his actor-observer role.

For example, when he reverses roles, he finds that he is observing himself while playing the part of another. When the director stops the action to interview the trainee in his new reversed role, the trainee is asked to share his perceptions and observations with others and to give these observations significance by verbalizing them. On a mechanistic or intellectual level the truly warmed-up participant forgets about the audience and his own life role. He becomes intensely involved in what is going on at the moment. However, from an emotional or psychological point of view, his life role and the audience observing him are never forgotten.

In a truly warmed-up group, the individual who moves into action, in a sense, represents the group. He might be thought of as bringing a part of the group with him when he moves into a roleplaying enactment. But the audience, too, is functioning on two levels. Obviously they are observers watching an interesting scene. But since the player, to some extent represents them, they are also emotionally involved in the action. At any time one of them might be called upon to enter into the scene either as a player or as an auxiliary to the protagonist. In a spontaneity training session where the focus is on action, group members gradually become aware of their function as actors *and* observers. Their role as judges or analysts is minimized. They begin to be able to move freely from the actor role to the observer role. Their ability to respond and react to their observations and at the same time observe and become more perceptive of their actions is enhanced. When this happens the two basic ingredients of spontaneity training are present: the individual becomes more sensitive, more perceptive, more aware of the forces present in human situations, and he becomes increasingly able to respond and react to these forces. If he becomes too preoccupied with analytical material and value judgments about his behavior, his ability to respond adequately will be constricted and inhibited. However, without role reversal, doubling, and soliloquy, he may well be so preoccupied with acting that he is unaware that his actions are inappropriate for the situation in which he finds himself. In utilizing the action approach to role training, a proper balance between the acting and observing functions must be maintained.

Surplus Reality

A second essential concept of spontaneity theory is *surplus reality*. A baseball player about to step into the batter's box, frequently picks up a practice bat filled with lead. He takes several swings with the bat, which is perhaps five times heavier than the one which he will actually use. Now when he picks up his regular bat it feels light and easy to handle. Analogously, in spontaneity training, group members observe more, feel more, and act more than life itself requires. Spontaneity training is perhaps the only form of dramatic activity where "overacting" is desirable. This essential ingredient of the action atmosphere encourages participants to try things they haven't tried before. It helps participants to free themselves from rigid patterns of behavior. Finally, it increases their capacity to deal with the "real thing."

Applications

If one views spontaneity as the ability to respond adequately to new situations and to respond in new and adequate

ways to old situations, then it becomes clear spontaneity training is useful in a great many situations. Whenever an individual
is dealing with one or more individuals in the changing situation typical of business activity, his ability to respond adequately to the nuances of behavior and situational forces which
surround him will, to a large extent, determine his value to his
company, his colleagues, and to himself. The capacity of the
individual to move about freely in his organizational and interpersonal relations often determines his effectiveness and frequently is the key to his own sense of well-being. Spontaneity
training is a process whereby the individual develops his ability
to respond and relate to other people more constructively, more
effectively, and more creatively.

Any attempt to catalogue applications of spontaneity training in industrial situations would amount to cataloguing the
entire range of interpersonal and organizational relationships
which exist in business today. It is in the application of spontaneity training that the idea of training "the whole man"
becomes a real and valid concept.

Therefore, in discussing roleplaying application in this
area, one must take a procedural point of view rather than
dealing with the content of the session. From the practitioner's
viewpoint, the content of the session is relatively unimportant;
the way in which he proceeds and the frame of reference
which he uses to guide and develop the session determine his
effectiveness. The basic procedure in applying roleplaying to
spontaneity training is described below:

First, the director warms up the group. This means that he
conducts a discussion, sets up a demonstration, or provides
some other stimulus for isolating the common ingredients of
the problem under consideration. He helps the group identify
and expose those aspects of the problem which must be dealt
with. If the roleplay is to be successful there must be a feeling

of commonality concerning the problem. It is not one individual's problem; rather it is a problem of mutual significance to the members of the group. It is here that the practitioner's approach departs significantly and profoundly from the approach used in method-centered roleplaying or in any didactic approach to teaching. For during the warm-up in a spontaneity training session the practitioner has no educational or training ax to grind. He has no training goal in the usual sense of a predetermined and clear cut objective toward which he will guide the group. His goal is to assist the group in isolating significant dimensions of the problem. In reaching this goal he cannot concern himself, or permit the group to concern itself, with "what's right" or "who's right." Rather the concern must be with what is, that is with the "here and now."

For example, in training foremen in handling grievances, the trainer may find that an individual in the group, after some discussion, blurts out: "I don't like union stewards." The director, rather than correcting the participant, or conducting a discussion to investigate the cause for his feelings, accepts what is said and attempts to tie it in with what has been said previously. If a second group member responds by saying: "That's ridiculous, after all, union stewards are human beings and some of them are good and some of them are bad," the practitioner does not try to resolve this conflict nor help the group to rationalize it. Rather he accepts the comment as a statement of feeling and conviction and again tries to establish commonality. Thus he might say: "Well, some of us feel that union people are no good, others feel that some are good and some are bad. Let's discuss a little further how we feel about the union steward." Now perhaps another participant will rise to the occasion and say: "I've found that with a union steward you should be firm, factual, and fair."

Again the director strives to achieve some commonality and

mutuality concerning the problem. He attempts to establish a group-centered feeling. So he says: "That's interesting. Tell us —how do you feel about these union people?" It may take five minutes, ten minutes, fifteen minutes, sometimes an entire session to focus attention on a common aspect of the problem which has significance and is acceptable to the total group. For example, in the union grievance training situation one can guess that at some point the individual group members might mutually draw the conclusion that: "There are times when it is difficult to deal with union stewards, they cause me problems, I wish I could find ways of getting along more effectively with them." In a sense the group in the warm-up phase of an action training session can be thought of as a pot of boiling water. As the water begins to boil, bubbles rise to the surface. Any premature attempt to rationalize these bubbles will sound the death knell for successful roleplaying enactments. But as the "pot boils," as feelings are expressed in an open and non-threatening atmosphere, and as the intensity of feelings increases, the group begins to approach a level of interest and commonality which sets the stage for action.

The most frequent error made by neophyte directors is their attempt to deal with every feeling, attitude, or opinion expressed. Thus, one group member has said "I don't like union stewards," another has said "You've got to be tough with them," someone else has presented an oversimplified generalization for dealing with every problem that arises. If the director attempts to deal with each of these statements, reconcile them, dig for causal forces, and in effect handle every bubble which rises to the surface, he'll find himself bogged down in a morass of conflicting attitudes and points of view. On the other hand, if he is guided by a firm and basic conviction that his goal is to get feelings out in the open regardless of what they are and patiently wait for an action situation with which to deal with them, he will have established a warmed-up atmosphere in which people can begin to experiment, interact, and become more spontaneous.

This is not to say that he should forget about participant's self-defeating or negative points of view but rather that they should be dealt with at the proper time. During the warm-up the director is concerned with getting feelings expressed, getting people involved and building some animation and interest into the discussion. The whole basis of roleplaying, in this context, is that the individual learns by doing, by becoming involved, and by becoming spontaneous. When sufficient interest and intensity of feeling have been established to hold the group together, then learning by doing can occur. The warmup is truly underway when each group member begins to think something like this: "This problem has real meaning for me. I remember specific situations in which I had difficulty in dealing with union members. Everyone else in this room has had some experiences which in some way are similar to mine. I want to talk about this, I want to hear what other peole have to say about it. I wonder what I can do to improve. There must be some better ways to handle this thing." When this occurs the group has been prepared for work, for action. When a member of the group moves to the front of the room to enact a situation of real significance to him, interest intensifies. When the director says: "Let's try to look at this problem from every possible angle," the group members nod in affirmation. If a group member is called upon to double or take an antagonist's role he moves into this situation with some feeling about what is going on. In this warm-up atmosphere the director can introduce action methods and the group will be receptive. There is no need for observer sheets, written outlines, notepaper or visual aids. The problem becomes real and meaningful to the group. Whatever is learned will be learned as a result of inter-action—it will be the result of a feeling experience rather than a mere intellectual exercise. And when one enactment is completed and others have experimented with dealing with the problem under consideration, there is no need to make a list of what should be done back on the job. For in the process of identifying with roleplayers, taking roles, and exchanging feelings group members have developed greater insight into the problem, they have become more aware of their own behavior and its impact on others.

A summary of postenactment discussion which follows role-playing scenes is not a critique or analysis of what happened. It is an exchange of feelings and insights. Thus one group member says: "You know, for the first time I realize that I feel very uncomfortable and nervous when the union steward comes to me with a complaint." And another member counters: "Yes, you know I think that's right, and when I was playing the role of the steward I began to feel how he must feel. I began to realize that it is unpleasant and uncomfortable for him, too." And someone else adds: "You know I've never really listened to what the steward has to say, to me he's always been just a pain in the neck." And so it goes, small insights, slightly increased awareness, a willingness to examine thoughts and feelings which heretofore remained unstated and unexamined. There are no clever summaries, no platitudes, no rules and regulations. Group members have become a little more understanding, a little more flexible, a little more able to look at themselves. For after all, an industrial training session does not convert the competitive, often rough-and-tumble, and frequently fraught-with-conflict industrial organization into a warm, friendly, understanding social agency. All that training can hope to do is to help people get along a little better.

Summary

Spontaneity training is training that has to do with feelings; it is training in which the act is more important than any predetermined value judgment; it shuns analysis. It is not concerned with what a man should do—it is concerned with what he can do—here and now.

APPENDIXES

Case Material

IN ROLEPLAYING one can distinguish two types of cases: (a) those made up on the spot, which one may label *spontaneous,* and (b) those prepared in advance, which may be labeled *contrived.*

In this section we shall present ten contrived or prepared cases which vary in *structure, format,* and *focus* to show how diverse may be the application of the technique. They are intended to be used in their present form but may be modified to suit special needs.

Structure

Structure refers to the amount of limiting information provided subjects. The less structure, the greater variations in the possibility of individual interpretation. For example, when a roleplayer is told only: "An employee will come to see you to talk about a problem," very little structure has been provided. When he is told in addition, "You are the personnel man, and among your duties is supervision of the employees' cafeteria," then more structure has been given. If additionally to this, the roleplayer is told, "The cafeteria was put under your supervision last week and you have asked employees to come to you with any suggestions," then it is evident that the situation is still more structured. Were more information given to the effect: "You are personally very much dissatisfied with how the cafeteria has been handled in the past and you want definite complaints so that you can make basic changes in menus and procedures," then the situation is further structured and gives the roleplayer more data in preparing for his role.

Suppose the instructions however, had been: "You are the personnel man and recently you have been put in charge of the employees' cafeteria. Employees need not eat in the cafeteria; they can bring in their lunches or eat at near-by restaurants. There is always a good deal of griping and complaining—and employees are coming to you, taking up your time with all kinds of stupid complaints." It is evident that since the roleplayer's instructions are quite different, the structure is changed.

Structuring permits the leader to direct the situation to particular ends, by giving roleplayers specific background information so that they can adapt themselves to particular elements. What degree of structuring is proper depends on the *purpose* of the roleplaying. For testing, the situation is usually relatively unstructured. In this way one can see how individuals interpret a role. In the example cited, the instructions: "You are a personnel man and recently you have been put in charge of the cafeteria" may be sufficient instructions if one wants to see how the individual will react to a vaguely structured situation. But if we are more interested in seeing how well a person will handle a more strictly delimited problem, more structure is introduced.

The same is true for the role of the antagonist or antagonists. For example, one might inform the antagonist: "The personnel director has asked every employee to come to see him if he has complaints about the cafeteria. Your major complaint is that it is too noisy. The reason being that there is no door between the kitchen and the dining-room. You believe that if a door is put up, this will improve matters." This amount of structure gives the employee enough information to know how to direct his statements. On the other hand, we could make the problem much vaguer simply by saying: "You will see the personnel man who is in charge of the cafeteria. You and many others have many complaints. You will try to explain some of the complaints to the personnel man, and see if you can get him to promise to correct them." These second instructions are now more vague in terms of a complaint, and more specific in terms of what the intensions of the antagonist are to be.

It must be kept in mind that structuring exists to various degrees—and that a situation may be structured to various amounts depending on what the director hopes to accomplish.

Format

By format is meant the particular procedures used. The situation may be of the "single" kind with one group role-playing before others or of the "multiple" type with a number of groups playing at the same time. The procedure may be of the "straight" type, or any of the various possible techniques such as "switching" may be utilized. There is no necessary virtue in any format variation. What is important is that the procedure used is appropriate to the group and useful for the director's intentions.

A director's skill is shown by his flexible use of appropriate format variations. Ordinarily, the simpler procedures are best, since complicated formats tend to confuse participants.

Focusing

Any roleplaying situation has a variable amount of meaning to individuals. Some problems may be of little interest or value to particular people or groups. Other situations may evoke intense interest. The wise director will utilize cases meaning-ful to the participants—to focus on their needs.

We can assume generality of needs for any homogeneous group, that whatever is meaningful for one individual tends to have meaning for the others. To the extent that the director can understand the needs of people and can diagnose their indi-vidual difficulties, he can develop problem situations that will be focused on their wants.

The Cases

In the subsequent pages we have developed a number of roleplaying cases intended to indicate various kinds of struc-ture, formats, and focusing. These cases can be used as they are: and have the advantage that they have been pretested and found to have general applicability. The director may wish to modify some of them for special purposes. It would be highly desirable, however, for the director to make up his own contrived cases, so that he can introduce suitable modifications designed to meet particular needs of the types of groups he works with.

There is some advantage for a director to have an arma-mentarium of familiar cases. In this manner he develops expe-rience with a particular situation, learns how to introduce it to a group, can learn a variety of approaches to the problem, and most of all, can now begin to compare any individual's solution against those of others.

Because we intend to demonstrate a wide variety of struc-tures, formats, and focusings, the cases differ considerably from each other in the three dimensions, and provide the director with more variations than he will ordinarily use. A good direc-tor, once he is secure in his ability to employ a particular format, should experiment with new procedures, so that he will finally arrive at the point where he can flexibly meet any group or individual needs in a rapid, spontaneous manner.

Case 1

Director's Notes

This is an example of a structured interrupted skit. The players read their parts in front of the group. In this way the two players and the members of the group get the structure of the situation. Then, suddenly the skit ends, but the problem is not solved. The players have to continue roleplaying in an effort to come to a satisfactory completion.

In making skits of this kind, attention must be given to length. In the present case, probably an optimal length is attained. Only enough information should be given to clarify the problem—and not enough to settle it. It may be noted in the present situation enough information is given to make the problem a tough one to solve: A has to think of three valid reasons and B cannot simply say "yes" or "no" to them.

This skit is probably best used for evaluation purposes to see how rapidly and how well people can think on their feet. Other skits can be made up that go into persistent problems. Such skits can lead training members into sensitive and ordinarily not-discussed problems.

Although such skits are ordinarily read for the first time on the stage, they may be examined by participants and prepared for in advance if desired.

A: Did you want to see me?
B: Sure, do sit down.
A: Thanks.

B: I suppose you know why I called you in?

A: I suppose it is about my resignation.

B: It took me by surprise. I know you were dissatisfied, but I didn't think you'd quit.

A: I discussed it with you.

B: That you were dissatisfied, I knew, but I told you I'd get around to your complaints.

A: Look—I don't want to sound angry or anything, but I told you about the problems six months ago, and you agreed then I had a point. Then I told you about them three months ago. Once again you told me personally that you'd do something about them. Finally, about a month ago I wrote them out. I have not heard from you. So, I figured you weren't going to do anything about them, so I handed in my resignation.

B: You're justified in quitting. But I hate to lose you. I don't think your resigning is good for you or for us. Now, you came down to three complaints about your job, am I right?

A: That's right. Just three.

B: Could you tell me them again?

A: What would be the use?

B: Honestly, I have been pretty busy and tied up. Maybe I have a tendency to let things slide, but right now I give you my word I'll listen carefully and give you immediate action if I think I can do something about them.

A: They're in my note to you.

B: It's five-thirty and my stenographer isn't in. I'll never find them. Do you remember them?

A: Of course I do.

B: Would you be so kind as to tell me what your three complaints are, and then we'll discuss them and I'll give you my answers and solutions.

A: I don't know what this would accomplish.

B: Have you really gotten another job?

A: No, I haven't. But in my field, well, you know as well as I, I won't have trouble getting something.

B: You are a good man. But if you haven't really gotten anything, what can you lose by telling me? And if I can rectify the problems, you'd be satisfied, wouldn't you?

A: I would.

B: Fine. Tell me then, one at a time, and I'll discuss them with you fully, and we'll settle them. If you are dissatisfied, let me know. I think I can satisfy you, however.

A: O.K. I shall be happy to tell you them, one at a time.

B: Right. One at a time we'll handle them. How long do you think this will take us?

A: About ten or fifteen minutes, no more.

B: Shoot: what is the first complaint you have about the job?

A: Well, it is . . .

(A *and* B *are to continue for about 10 to 15 minutes*)

Case 2

Director's Notes

This is an example of a structured case intended to develop particular skills. This case is particularly useful with multiple groups playing the problem simultaneously. You will note how important it is to use an observer, who is given a number of items to look out for.

After the acting, if multiple roleplaying is used, the various observers can combine their criticisms and comments in the discussion. After the discussion, new teams can be formed and the situation can be replayed. (For example, all those who played the role of Willard Rogers can now play the role of Frank Wilcox; and the Wilcoxes can now play the role of observers, and the former observers can now play the role of Willard Rogers.) Or, since how one uses these cases calls for flexibility, one may ask observers to rate the various people, and a highly-rated Willard Rogers may then replay his part before the group; or a volunteer Willard Rogers can do this, especially someone who feels his performance was inadequate.

The most general use of this variation is to train people in specific procedures, and to get them to see themselves in a more comprehensive manner.

Instructions for Willard Rogers

You are a salesman for the J. C. Food Co. Your company is putting on a big push on Quickie Instant Orange Juice. Here are some of the selling points:

1. Quickie is more concentrated than competitors' brands. You get almost one full glass more when you buy Quickie. It costs about one cent more per can, but the housewife saves money on every can she buys.

2. There is strong national advertising support on T.V. and in the newspapers for this new brand. The retail customers will be looking for it.

Your immediate goal is to get your customer to install an attractive point-of-purchase display. The display was scientifically tested in other cities, and increased orange juice sales as much as 30%. Mr. Wilcox, the store manager whom you will talk to has already agreed to purchase one case of Quickie. If he accepts the display, then you should see whether you can get him to take on an additional case, since sales will be more rapid.

Mr. Wilcox will give you the usual nominal opposition, but will permit you to make your pitch.

Instructions for Frank Wilcox

You now own your own retail grocery, after seven years of working for a big chain. Your profits are good, and you are aware that your success depends mostly on your being a smart merchandiser. Every salesman who comes to see you routinely tries to sell you more merchandise than you can use; and almost every one of them wants you to display his merchandise "up front." They frequently have some gimmick or other. You don't like too many displays because they clutter up the store, but every once in a while, if a display is tastefully done,

175

you do permit one to be set up. Another reason you don't particularly like displays is that you frequently run sales of your own and you want to push your own special items.

You agreed a week ago to purchase one case of Quickie Instant Orange Juice from the salesman, Willard Rogers. You figure it won't hurt to give this brand a try, even though you are already carrying three brands of orange juice. Quickie costs you a penny more per can, and you will have to sell it at a penny more per can to customers. You are told that Quickie makes five instead of four glasses of orange juice, and this is a salespoint that will be stressed in television and newspaper ads. So, despite your reluctance to put in a new brand, which causes you more trouble in warehousing, you have decided to try out one case to see how well it sells.

One thing about yourself: you don't like it when a salesman tries to make up your mind and tell you what is best for your store: if they know so much they should be in business for themselves. Right now you have enough free time to talk with Willard Rogers, and you want to keep his friendship but not let him sell you unless he really has a good proposition.

Instructions for Observer

Please read the instructions of Willard Rogers and Frank Wilcox. This will outline the problem to be enacted. It shall be your function to note what goes on, the good and the poor points made by both men, but pay special attention to Willard Rogers. Check for these points:

1. Rogers' opening remarks. What attitude does he convey? Does he establish a favorable atmosphere?
2. Rogers' ability to get hidden objections out in the open.
3. How well does Wilcox handle Rogers' various points?

4. What techniques does Rogers use to meet Wilcox's rather reluctant attitude?

5. How well does Rogers present his sales points?

6. What impression does Rogers create on Wilcox?

7. How was the closing of the sale made?

In addition to these seven points be ready to comment on any other elements you may notice in the interview.

Case 3

Director's Notes

Situation 3 ordinarily causes a great deal of tension and anxiety in all participants. It involves three people each of whom get instructions to operate in certain ways the others do not expect. It is a two-stage problem. Mr. Smart who is to go to see Mr. Bigg has first to see Leslie, Mr. Bigg's secretary. The treatment of Mr. Smart by Leslie usually throws off Mr. Smart, and the unexpected treatment of Mr. Bigg further upsets him. It is not unusual, when the situation is well played to find Mr. Smart blowing up.

For these reasons, Situation 3 is a powerful one for understanding how the person who plays Mr. Smart can react to disappointments and to frustrations. It also indicates how Leslie can handle a very unpleasant assignment and how Mr. Bigg deals with a delicate task.

None of the three participants are to know the others' instructions. They should read their parts to themselves; or if they are to get structure publicly, the director should read the parts to each one in front of the group, while the other two participants are out of the room.

Mr. Bigg and Leslie can be seated back to back. Mr. Bigg is in another office and can not "hear" what Smart and Leslie are saying.

Almost anything can happen in this situation, and it is an excellent attention getter.

Instructions for Leslie

Your name is Leslie and you are secretary to Mr. Bigg, president of the Bigg Realty Company. You have a good boss in Mr. Bigg; he pays well, and he is very considerate. However, he has his peculiarities. He does not like to be interrupted with calls or visits while he is working, and likes to have a schedule. A great many people try to see him, especially salesmen. It is your job to make appointments for these people. At the end of the day you tell him who came, what they want, and whom they represent, and then he decides if he wants to see them.

Mr. Bigg is especially sensitive about insurance men. They use all kinds of tricks to try to get in to see him.

A Mr. Smart will come in to see Mr. Bigg. You will take his name, address, business connection, and purpose of his visit. You will give him an appointment for the next day—if you can. He will probably be very persistent. You explain your instructions, and see if you can get him to come in tomorrow. Tell him you cannot interrupt Mr. Bigg, but you will let him know at the end of the day—about 5 p.m. (it is now 2 p.m.) that Mr. Smart called.

If you are able to discourage Mr. Smart and get him to leave, *call him back*, go into Mr. Bigg's office and tell him Mr. Smart is outside. If you are not able to discourage Mr. Smart *in three minutes*, then go to Mr. Bigg's office and tell him Mr. Smart wishes to see him. Mr. Bigg will be sitting with his back to you, but he is in another office and cannot hear what is going on in your office.

Instructions for Joe Bigg

Your name is Joe Bigg. You are president of the Bigg Realty Company which your late father established. You are an up-and-coming person in this town: a member of the city council, a trustee of the Middletown Country Club, and there is mention of nominating you for mayor. Your wife would be extremely happy if you became mayor because there is some talk that you are a success only because your father started the business.

You are in your office. Your secretary sees all visitors, and has orders to not disturb you. You like to plan your day and like to have appointments made in advance.

Yesterday, to your surprise, you saw Jim Smart in the street. You hadn't seen him for 15 years. He had been your best friend when you were kids. He was a bit wild in those days and used to get you into all kinds of minor troubles. Your mother didn't like him and she used to say: "He's smart all right; smart in all ways." Jim once saved your life when you were swimming in the lake. Well, Jim told you he had been in the army and now was thinking of settling down in Middletown. You told him to drop in to see you at the office whenever he could.

Last night, at the country club you mentioned running into Jim, and found out that everybody remembered him—and nobody liked him. They all felt it would be a good thing if he stayed out of town. Some of the people felt that he might even be a little crooked. You were surprised to find how much he was disliked.

Jim will drop in to see you today. Your problem is to tell

him as tactfully as possible that it would not be a good thing for him to settle in Middletown. Tell him that there are too many insurance men now, that the town has changed, and so forth. After all, in view of the attitude of others about Jim, his presence will embarrass you. Be polite but firm. See if you can sell him on the idea of not coming to Middletown.

When Jim enters he will see your secretary, Leslie. You will not know he has come until your secretary enters your office to tell you that Jim is here. She has orders to discourage visitors, and maybe he will just go away.

Instructions for Jim Smart

Your name is Jim Smart. You grew up in Middletown. Fifteen years ago you left to go into the army and then you went to college. Ten years ago you got married and now have two children. You settled down in the big city and went into insurance, and you have done fairly well. However, you always wanted to return to Middletown—it is an ideal place to bring up a family. You are now back in Middletown, and you are looking around. This is a good place to live and you are almost sure you will want to open an office here. There are not many insurance people in town, and you may really make a success of it here.

Yesterday, on the street, you met Joe Bigg. He was your best friend in High School. He graduated only because you helped him with his math. Both of you had lots of fun together, and once you saved his life while swimming. You talked only briefly with Joe because you had an appointment at the bank, and he told you his father died and that now he was the head of the Bigg Realty firm. *He was cordial to you and asked you to drop in to see him in his office if you wished.*

Last night you found out that Joe Bigg is now one of the most important men in town. His realty company is the biggest; he is on the city council and is slated to become the mayor and he is a trustee of the country club to which all the important people in town belong, and there would be no point in your settling down here unless you were a member of the country club.

This is your problem: it is now 2 p.m. You have another appointment at 3 p.m. You are going to catch a plane at 4:30 back to your family in the big city. You will enter Joe Bigg's office and will see his secretary and you will ask to see Joe and will talk with him. Tell him you have decided to settle down in Middletown. *See if you can get him to agree to present your name for membership in the country club.*

Your task is to see if you can get him to suggest it; if not, bring it up yourself. Get a firm answer one way or another, because unless you will get into the country club, there would be little point in coming to Middletown.

Joe will be in his office, in another "room" and can not hear you while you are talking to the secretary.

Case 4

Director's Notes

Situation 4 is complex with a good deal of structuring of the attitudes of five people: Jim Rule, the production manager; Old Mr. Tom Brown, one of the founders of Brown and Green Manufacturing Company, president and semiretired; his son Wally Brown, vice-president in charge of personnel; Sam Green, son of Joe Green, now deceased; and Joe Plenty, retired production manager.

Each of these five people have their private attitudes about Jim's autonomy.

Each of them has a position to maintain, which differs to some extent from that of the others. The problem is to see how well each of the individuals can make his various points about Jim Rule's autonomy and how well the group as a whole can come up with a good solution to the company's problems.

Each of the players should be given sufficient time to read and think over the situation. It might be well, if possible, to let each person study his role for at least a day, rehearsing it to himself.

Instructions for Jim Rule

Your name is Jim Rule, and this is your story.

You grew up in Middletown and, after finishing high school, you went to work as a machine apprentice at the Brown and Green Manufacturing Company. You entered the Air Force during the war and came out four years later. You graduated from an engineering school, and went to work at Brown and Green as a junior engineer. Seven years later, you were promoted to head engineer, and supervised four other engineers. Three years later, after Joe Plenty, production chief retired, you got his job—at a salary almost twice what you were making as chief engineer. Not only did you believe you were the proper man for the job, but so did everyone else.

However, in the year you have been production manager, things have not worked out well. First, there were too many accidents and too many rejects. Then, there was a flash strike —for no apparent reason. Also, there has been too much interference. First, Old Man Brown, who is president, but who is really semiretired, tries to run the plant as he did when there were twenty employees. Now there are 400. You resent his going over your head, giving orders in contradiction to yours. Then there is Wally Brown, the son of Old Mr. Brown and vice-president in charge of personnel. He is meeting-happy, and calls conferences usually at the worst possible times. There is a lot of talk, most of it useless. Then there is Sam Green, the son of Joe Green, one of the original founders, always interfering with your production. He sells things you don't have, and insists they have to be made. This interferes with your scheduling. And then there is old Joe Plenty, who was your former boss and had your present job. He comes into the mill about twice a week, taking up your time with reminiscences and he talks with the older workers, most of whom are still loyal to him, and keeps them from working.

You are pretty disturbed about the situation, and would like to quit. Your wife, who grew up in Middletown will not hear of moving, and advises you to learn how to get along better with the others. Actually, you could not find as good a job anywhere else, and if only they would leave you alone, everything would go well.

Today Wally is calling another meeting. His father, old Mr. Brown, who has just come back from a six months' vacation in Florida, will be there as well as the others. It is your intention to tell them you can't really do your job unless they let you alone. Specifically, this is what you want:

1. Mr. Brown should not give orders in your department over your head. He should give them to you and not to your foremen.

2. Wally Brown should stop interfering with your work. One meeting every two weeks should be enough.

3. Sam Green should discuss new orders with you to see whether you can put them out on time. Many times you have to work yourself and your men overtime and still you can't meet the deadlines.

4. Joe Plenty shouldn't come into the mill during working hours. He is a disturbing influence on the men.

Instructions for Thaddeus Brown

You are Thaddeus Brown, one of the founders of Brown and Green Manufacturing Company. You are president, but you are semiretired. You have just come back from a six months' stay in Florida, and you are going to attend a meeting of the top men of the company including your son Wally, who is vice-president in charge of personnel and Sam Green, who is the son of your deceased partner. Sam is now vice-president in charge of sales. Also, your old friend Joe Plenty will be there. Joe is a stockholder in the company, formerly was Production Chief, the job that Jim Rule now has, and he is now retired. He is a member of the board of directors, and he still has an active interest in the company.

You have seen the company going up and down. In the last several years, things have been doing well. You have a good team. Your best man is Jim Rule, who has been with the company a long time, who was formerly Chief Engineer and now is Production Head.

You have been thinking things over, and you have decided you have been interfering too much with Jim. Also, you know Joe Plenty has been putting his nose in Jim's business too much. Jim is an excellent engineer, a very ambitious and hard working person, with a lot of drive. You wish this were true about your son Wally, who is filled with a lot of fancy ideas.

It is your intention to say that you will not interfere any longer with Jim Rule's work, and that from now on you want to make major decisions only, and not give orders. You also think that Joe Plenty should lay off Jim Rule, who is rather touchy about his authority. Joe has a lot of friends in the shops, some of whom are still loyal to him, and Jim resents this. Sam is a kind of playboy, but a good salesman, but he doesn't really understand Jim's problems, and he should co-ordinate his selling to the Mill's potentials.

You like Jim Rule and you think he is really the best bet to become president when you retire in a couple of years. There have been some frictions, and you'd like to settle things. You will come to the meeting which you will lead with the intention of letting each person have his full say about company problems and then see if you can get everybody to come to a good understanding.

Instructions for Wally Brown

You are Wally Brown, son of Thaddeus Brown, a founder of the Brown and Green Manufacturing Company. Your father is president, and he will probably retire in a year or two. You are vice-president in charge of personnel, and the most likely candidate to be the president when your father retires. Sam Green, son of your father's deceased partner, is vice-president in charge of sales. Sam is a playboy, but a good salesman. He is usually in trouble with Jim Rule, the new Production Head. Jim is a good man, an able engineer, but does not know how to get along with people. He is not a very good production man, because he is strictly a slide-rule engineer. What he needs is better understanding of human relations, to know how to deal more tactfully with people, and you think the very best thing for him would be to take a management course. He was a pilot in the Air Force and is really a brilliant engineer, but because of his brusque manners, has created a lot of hostility. The people in the shops don't like him, and it is a good thing Joe Plenty, the former Production Head comes around to smooth things over when there is trouble. There was a flash strike a couple of months ago, and if it weren't for Joe, there would have been a general walkout. The men don't like Jim's manners. He also fights with Sam, who tries his best to get orders for the firm.

It is your well considered opinion, and you have talked this over with Sam, that Jim ought to take off a couple of months and go to some management school. Joe could take over for the time being as Production Head. You are pretty sure he would like it, and the men would, too. Joe is a calm, wise old man and knows how to deal with people.

Jim does not like you too much. He resents the meetings you call, which are mainly intended to help him understand better what he is doing. You think, however, he is right in one of his complaints, which he made secretly once to you—your father does go over his head too much. As a matter of fact your father hires and fires people, which should be your responsibility.

Your major idea at this meeting you are calling, which your father will preside over, is that Jim ought to take a course in management and human relations techniques.

Instructions for Sam Green

You are Sam Green, vice-president in charge of sales of Brown and Green Manufacturing Company. Your father was one of the founders. He is now dead. Old Thaddeus Brown, the other partner, is president, but is semiretired. The organization is run mostly by Wally Brown, Thaddeus Brown's son, who is vice-president in charge of personnel, Jim Rule, Production Head, and yourself. At your staff meetings, Joe Plenty, a major stockholder and member of the board frequently attends. Joe, who was formerly Production Head is a wise old man and in your opinion was chiefly responsible for the company's early growth.

Here is how you see the situation. Jim Rule is just not fit for his job as production head. Sure, he is a good engineer, but he really doesn't know how to deal with people, and gets them angry by his manner. He is very tactless with you and just cannot understand that the company depends on orders.

No matter how you approach him, he bristles and seems to think every order is an insult to him.

Old Mr. Brown should have retired long ago. He still tries to run the plant as he did forty years ago. Wally Brown is filled with a lot of strange ideas, and is meeting-happy. Old Joe Plenty is a good man, and if you could get another man like him then there would be no trouble with production. You are a good salesman: everybody admits that.

Here is how you size up the situation.

Old Mr. Brown ought to retire. Or, at least, he shouldn't be interfering with everybody else.

Jim Rule should go back into engineering. He just doesn't have what it takes to be Production Chief. It would be quite a drop in salary, but the company's interests come first.

Joe Plenty should take over production again until a new production chief is hired; or maybe, he should come back as advisor, and maybe Jim Rule would learn how to deal with people better. You doubt this, however. You have nothing against Jim. You just don't think he has it.

As far as Wally is concerned, you think he should stick to his personnel work. He isn't much of an asset to the company in any way.

Instructions for Joe Plenty

Your name is Joe Plenty. You were the first employee of Brown and Green Manufacturing Company, and last year after forty years of service you retired because you felt that the company needed a younger man. You invested heavily in the company, and you have about 10 per cent of the shares now, and are the third largest stockholder.

For twenty years you were Production Head, and when you retired you suggested Jim Rule succeed you. He is a brilliant, hard working, ambitious person, a bit too stiff and a bit too driving, but he has a good head on his shoulders and you think he will go a long way and is the most likely candidate for the presidency of the firm.

You like Jim, although he is quite sensitive about your coming to the factory. You try as tactfully as you can to give him pointers about running the factory, and you think he really appreciates them, although, being young and ambitious, he probably doesn't think he needs them as much as he really does. You also have calmed down some of the older men who resent him, and it was you who stopped a recent flash strike. You have continually supported him. He has had more than his share of the bad breaks during the year he has been Production Head, and Old Mr. Brown, president, took this past year as an opportunity to do things he wouldn't have done when you were Production Head. Also, that young Mr. Wally Brown, old man Brown's son is full of funny ideas, and he too interferes with Jim. And of course there is smart Sam Green, the son of the former partner, now head of sales, and he is always trying to make trouble for Jim.

Old Mr. Brown is back from his vacation (which you suggested, by the way), to discuss giving Jim some freedom, and Wally has called another meeting, which you shall attend.

Here is how you size up the situation:

Jim Rule is a good man, and the others should lay off him.

Thaddeus Brown ought to think of retiring soon.

Wally Brown ought to mind his own business, and just hire and fire men.

Sam Green should be considerate of Jim in writing orders and he should have an understanding of Jim's problems. After all now, with unions and all kinds of government restrictions, one can't be as flexible as one could in the old days.

Thaddeus Brown will run the meeting, and your usual

procedure is to shut up and listen, and when everybody else is pretty run down, you give your ideas and make your suggestions.

Case 5

Director's Notes

This situation is unique since it requires no prior structuring of the main participant, and also in that while it is an interactional situation the assistant does not appear, and has a minimal part to play.

This situation tests the quick thinking of the participant and also gives considerable information about him. But mostly it establishes the participant's capacity to summarize succinctly and clearly what he thinks of himself.

The participant is to be told the following:

"You are at home, alone. It is a Sunday evening. The telephone will ring, and you shall answer it. Imagine that the telephone is at your elbow. You will get all other information over the telephone."

In the meantime, an assistant is given a sheet of paper with the instructions for Case 5. At the signal from the director, the assistant makes a ringing sound to simulate a telephone bell, and then he reads off his lines. If a dummy telephone is readily available, or even a toy phone, it will be of value.

Instructions for Assistant

On a signal, make a telephone-ringing sound. Mr. ——— will then answer the telephone. After he says "hello" you say (slowly and distinctly), "This is Colonel Peter Bell calling from Washington, D. C., in reference to the Office of Strategic

Services. You have been suggested for an assignment of considerable importance to the welfare of this country. I cannot tell you the nature of this matter, and all I want is some information about you. (Pause.) Are you willing to give it to me? (Pause. Mr. ——— may say "Yes," in which case go on to the material in the next paragraph. In case he hesitates, inform him that the question you wish to ask will be general—and about himself. Should he wish to call you back tell him to call the Office of Strategic Service in Washington, and you will answer. In any event, get him to answer the question.)

"Before I tell you the question, let me tell you that it is a test, designed to see how well you can answer the question. Our conversation is being recorded on a tape recorder, and you will have exactly five minutes to answer it. I cannot repeat any of the questions, and I will not answer any questions you may have. Are you ready?" (After you get his assent, say:) "This is the question: Tell me all about yourself in five minutes: personal history, educational history, social history, and employment history. I shall tell you when the five minutes are up. Don't begin until I say 'Now'." (Wait ten full seconds, and then say:) "Now!" (Look at your watch, and at the end of five minutes say:) "Stop! That is all, Mr. ———, thank you."

Case 6

Director's Notes

This is an example of a complicated roleplaying case, in that it has no less than four separate scenes. (1) The president reads off a statement to a consultant. (2) Then the consultant has an interview with the foreman, who now relays certain information to him. (3) Then the consultant meets with the foreman and the workers. (4) The consultant then meets again with the president to give his report.

Each of the seven people in the situation have their separate instructions. While the major purpose of this scene is to test the consultant's capacity to find a proper solution to the problem (there are a number of possible solutions) it is no less a test of the other individuals who are to present their points of view as plausibly as possible.

Instructions for the President

You are a *very* busy man. You will let Bob Lonergan, the industrial consultant who is coming to see you know this. You will give him no more than *three minutes* of your time. You don't even know his name and don't care to know it. Tell him simply the following: "There's a problem going on down in the plant. I want you to meet Mr. Sanderson, the foreman, who will tell you what it is. Talk it over with him and the men involved and come up with some solution. Come back with the foreman to see me as soon as you have figured out a solution." After this, call in Mr. Sanderson and introduce the two men and leave. Later, Mr. Lonergan and Mr. Sanderson will come back to see you.

Instructions for the Foreman

You have been having a lot of trouble with your men about a particular problem. The president told you he would hire a consultant to solve the problem. When the president introduces you to the consultant, don't tell him what the problem is. Tell him only that he has to come and see for himself since you don't want to prejudice him in any way. Be very firm about this. You never met this consultant before, and you don't even know his name.

Then, take him to the men, introduce him, and try to keep out of the discussion as much as possible. Agree with the men as much as you can. When the discussion is over, and the consultant goes back to the president, you go along with him, as the president told you, and when the consultant gives his advice, try to knock as many holes in it as you can.

Instructions for the Consultant

You have been called in by Mr. Harvey Brown to act as a consultant for a problem he has in his plant. You have never met Mr. Brown and have never been in the plant before. This is what will happen to you:

1. You will meet the president, who will tell you something about the problem.
2. Then you will be introduced to the foreman, whose men are causing the trouble, and you will try to get more information out of him.
3. Then you will meet with the foreman and the workers, and will get further information. You will try to work out a solution to the problem. You will try to get agreement from everybody that this is a good solution.
4. You will then return, with the foreman to Mr. Brown, the president, and you will give him your recommended solution.

Instructions for Art Baker

You work with Bill Cable, Chuck Donnelly, and Don Brown. Don is not in today. There has been a lot of trouble in the department, and the foreman has not been able to solve the problem. You understand the company is going to hire a consultant to come to a solution. You will try to tell him in front of the foreman and the other men just how you see things, and what the right answer should be.

You are the first man in the process. The work comes to

you first. You set it up so that Bill can work on it. You have to go with your hand truck to another department to get it, and frequently there are only one or two pieces, and when this happens it means you have to make a lot of trips. If at the other department they would have full loads for you then you wouldn't have to make so many trips, since you can easily carry twenty pieces at a time. You think the other department should keep a stockpile, and keep ahead of you. You have other things to do, such as packing final items, keeping the work room clean, and you don't think it right for you to keep running back and forth all the time with one or two pieces. Bill gets pretty angry when there isn't any work for him. As you see it, it is the foreman's fault that he doesn't make Don Brown, who isn't in today, keep ahead of you.

Instructions for Bill Cable

You are on piece work. The work is brought to you by Art Baker, who is supposed to keep you supplied. Whenever you ask Art to get the material he grumbles and tells you to wait a while. He claims he has a lot of other things to do, and hates to go to the other department to Don Brown for work unless he can come with a filled truck. Sometimes you have gone yourself to get material, and you have found more than a truckfull. The other department is also run by the foreman. Don Brown is not in today, because he is sick. You think that if Don could signal Art whenever he has enough work for you then there would be no trouble.

Another fellow who gives you trouble is Chuck Donnelly. He complains the chips from your work land on him, and sometimes get in his eyes. This is true, but you can't help it. The room you work in is small, and you work face to face with Chuck, and when you are working you can't always be careful. Chuck ought to wear glasses or something.

Instructions for Chuck Donnelly

There is too much arguing between Art Baker and Bill Cable. Bill is always asking Art to go to Don Brown in another department to get work for him. Art hates to go unless there is a full load waiting for him. If Don kept a stock pile, there would always be enough work for him to give to Art to take to Bill. Also, Bill is careless and sends chips all over you. You had to go to the plant nurse twice last month to take things out of your eyes. Safety glasses are not really needed and they make you feel pretty bad. You'd rather quit than use them. Maybe they ought to put up a glass screen between you and Bill.

Instructions for Don Brown

You will come in late to work today, because you weren't feeling well. However, you get information that a consultant is coming in to the shop to discuss a problem. The problem affects you. This is the problem. You do work on some objects, and when you finish them put them down. Then Art Baker comes, takes them to another room where Bill Cable works on them. Sometimes you pile up a lot of work and Art does not come and you have no place to put them, so you have to take his truck and cart and take them to Bill yourself. Sometimes Art comes and there are no pieces or only a couple and he gets angry with you because he had to make a trip. If you had more space, so you could keep about 100 pieces waiting, that would be a solution, then you could always keep well ahead of Art. Also, if there were some way to let Art know when you are ready that would be a good thing.

(You will enter the room when the director gives you a signal. Your foreman's name is Jim Sanderson.)

194

Case 7

Director's Notes

A problem for roleplaying may be read out to a group so that everyone understands his own role and that of everyone else. Case 7 is of this kind.

The director should proceed as follows: ask for five volunteers, or if the group is large for two or more sets of five volunteers. To each group there may be assigned one or more observers. Then, without further explanation one person in each group is assigned the role of Bill Black, another the role of Dan Black, George Sims, Sid Johns, and Pat Carey. When every person knows his own "name" the director should read aloud the "story" of this group. Then, the group or groups are asked to go ahead and work out the problem. At the end of about 15-20 minutes, they are told they must come to some decisions in five minutes. After an additional five minutes, the meeting is ended, and the observers report on decisions.

It now can become the problem of the entire group to analyze the small group behavior of each individual, and, if two or more groups simultaneously meet, to try to discover why different decisions occurred in each group.

"The Acme Manufacturing Company has a staff meeting the last Tuesday of every month. Today the following five people shall be present: Bill and Dan Black, who are brothers, George Sims, production manager, Sid Johns, sales manager, and Pat Carey, personnel man and training director. Bill and Dan are co-owners of the Acme Manufacturing Company. Bill is the senior partner and shall run the meeting. He has no vote in any decision, but he does contribute his opinions.

"Dan, who is retired, believes that training is a waste of time, and that Pat Carey's assistant who spends his time exclusively doing training, should be fired, or spend his time doing personnel work. He feels the company, which has 200 employees, does not need a training program.

"George Sims, who is the production manager thinks he should become a vice-president. He has spent 18 years with the company. He believes that the training program is valuable and has paid off in higher production and fewer accidents. He also feels that Sid Johns, the sales manager, should check with him before accepting any new contracts, and should not agree to supply special orders.

"Sid Johns also wishes to become a vice-president, in charge of sales, and has no opinion about training. He does think, however, that Pat Carey should do a better job of recruiting personnel, especially a better quality of salesmen. He is convinced that expansion of the company depends on sales and any special services pay off in the long run.

"Pat Carey has been offered a new job with a larger salary, and thinks he should get a ten per cent raise which would be equivalent to the new salary. If his assistant should be let go, he would resign. He is in urgent need of a secretary to help him and his assistant, who has been doing an excellent job.

"All five of these people have discussed each of these various issues in the past. Bill Black is quite eager that some real decisions be made today. The group has ——— minutes to come to some decisions. Five minutes before the end of the meeting, I will give you a signal that time is almost up."

Case 8

Director's Notes

Case 8 represents a common type of problem in industry: a supervisor has to make decisions which affect a number of people and in order to come to the most equitable solution, he calls in the individuals to see what is the most satisfactory compromise that can be made.

In this problem's enactment, it is good to break up the observers into subgroups to examine and report on the behavior of the individuals. If a number of groups work on this problem (multiple roleplaying), one observer can be assigned to each group, and he will report on all members. The reporters, the roleplayers, and the supervisor each are given separate instructions which should be typed out on cards which each person reads at the same time and independently of the others, so each person understands only his own situation.

In the evaluation, the behavior of the supervisor is most important. Among the various items to look for would be the efficiency of the groups, etc., as noted in the instructions for the observers.

Frequently, this type of problem can run for a considerable length of time, but ordinarily ten minutes is enough to come to fairly good conclusions. The director may, if he finds differences between supervisors, ask a high-rated supervisor to conduct a group before the rest of the audience (usually having new people to work with) and the group as a whole can then observe and analyze his behavior.

Instructions for Supervisor

You have six people working under you: Al (or Alberta if a female), Bob (or Bobbie), Carl (or Carla), Dan (or Danica), Ernest (or Ernestine), and Francis (or Frances). Yesterday you got a note from your personnel director which reads as follows:

Dear Henry:

Vacations this year will be in the months of July, August, and September. Each of the six employees you supervise is to have two weeks vacation, preferably to prevent payroll trouble, on consecutive weeks. Do not schedule more than one person out at any time so as not to affect production schedules. Send me your list of employees and their vacation dates as soon as possible. I'd suggest you discuss this with the entire group so as to make the best possible scheduling, and with the least amount of difficulty.

Sincerely yours,

John Super

Here are some facts: this is the first time you have discussed vacations with this group. You have to make decisions today. You will try if possible, to come to the best solution.

Al is 62 years old and has been with the company 15 years.

Bob is 45 years old and has been with the company 20 years.

Carl is 40 years old and has been with the company 17 years.

Dan is 38 years old and has been with the company 20 years.

Ernest is 35 years old and has been with the company 2 years.

Francis is 29 years old and has been with the company 8 years.

Instructions for Al

You are 62 years old and have been with the company for 15 years. For more than 30 years you have vacationed the first two weeks in July at a summer camp. There you have met with your friends and family. Last year because of scheduling problems for vacations you went the second and third weeks, which you didn't like at all. You have strict orders from your wife to fight for your rights and to take your vacation the first two weeks in July. If this is not possible, then the second and third weeks are acceptable. You have already rented your cabin at the lake, and if you have to change your vacation, this means you may lose your deposit. You are the oldest worker in your particular work group, but you have only five years of seniority. Only Ernest, who is 35 years old has less seniority than you.

Instructions for Bob

You are 45 years old and have 20 years of seniority. Only Al is older than you, and only Dan has as much seniority as you. You would prefer to have your vacation the first two weeks of July, because this is usually the hottest part of summer. However, if others want this period badly, you are willing to take the next two weeks in July.

Instructions for Carl

You are 40 years old, and have been with the company for 17 years. Al and Bob are older than you and only Bob and Dan have more seniority. You'd like to take your vacation in July especially the second two weeks; if not then the first two weeks in August. You might even take them in the last two weeks of August, but September is out because you have school-age kids and they have to be back in school in September.

Instructions for Dan

You are 38 years old and have 20 years of seniority in the company. If vacations come up, you feel that you and Bob have first and equal say, since you both have the same amount of seniority. Your in-laws are going to stay with you the first two weeks in July, so you will not want that period. You have schoolchildren so you don't want to take your vacation off in September. It would be all right with you to take the last two weeks off in July or possibly any two weeks in August.

Instructions for Ernest

You are 35 years old and have only two years of seniority, less than anyone else in your work group. You and your wife have already made plans to go to a summer hotel the first two weeks in September, when the rates are a bit lower.

Instructions for Francis

You are 29 years old, the youngest worker in your group, but you have eight years of seniority. Ernest and Al have less seniority than you. You would like to have your vacation during the first two weeks in August, if you cannot get it in July which you prefer. If your vacation comes in September, you will not be able to go away unless you can get the first two weeks because school for your two kids starts September 15.

Instructions for Observer

Your main task is to observe the individual assigned to you: it may be Henry Foreman, the foreman of the group, whose problem is to set up a vacation schedule, or one of the other six people who are affected.

If you are assigned to observe the whole group notice the good and the poor things each person does, writing down any comments you have. Henry's main task is to get a quick, reasonable sensible, peaceful solution. Each of the other individual's have certain demands, and it should be of interest to you to note how they make out.

Compile a final list, and after any decision has been made,

you may query the various people to see how satisfied they are with their various vacation assignments.

Case 9

Director's Notes

This is a somewhat complicated case utilizing two participants and their Inner Selves—Ned Newman, a new employee, and Mr. Form, his foreman. Newman and Form learn their roles right on the stage since their Inner Selves explain their roles to Form and Newman in front of the group. The procedure is as follows:

1. Obtain four individuals. Mr. Form and Mr. Newman are to go on the stage. They are told that their Inner Selves will clarify the situation, and that once they know what their problem is they can begin roleplaying. The two Inner Selves are given scripts, which they are to read to their Real Selves (Form and Newman) successively on the stage in such manner that all can hear.

2. The Inner Selves, as indicated in the instructions, successively take their real selves out of the room. They should be given time to read and study their parts.

3. The Director may ask the observers to break into two groups—to observe Newman and Form.

Instructions for Form's Inner Self

You are the inner self of Mr. Form. You will read the material below to Mr. Form, *standing behind him*. Read slowly and clearly. After you finish, leave the room and take Mr. Form with you. As soon as you go out Mr. Newman and his Inner Self will come into the room. The director will later ask both of you to come back. When you return, you'll sit down and watch the action between Newman and Form.

"My name is Mr. Form—F-O-R-M, and I am a foreman. I am anxious to do a good job. I have been foreman for six months.

"Yesterday Mr. Super, my boss called me in. 'Form,' he said, 'There is too much lateness going on, also too many people are out on coffee breaks and they stay out too long. I want you to run a tight shop here. It is your responsibility to make sure people come in on time and give the company the time they are getting paid for. I want to have you talk to them, especially the new men, like that Ned Newman. Now Ned's only been around for about two weeks and already he is coming in late. Can you talk to him and straighten him out?'

"I told Mr. Super: 'Sure, but you know the older men come in late, and they have been doing it a long time. I think we should start with them.'

"Well, I don't like it. I think what's right for one is right for all. But that is my job. I got to do what I am told. So, this morning I came in at 8:30 and sure enough Ned Newman wasn't in yet. So I left a note on his time card to come see me as soon as he came in. It is a quarter to nine already, and he isn't in yet. I am now in my office, and when he comes in, I am going to put it on the line and tell him as nicely but as firmly as possible that he must come in on time if he wants to work here, and that is all there is to it. I am waiting for him. It is now 8:46, and he is still not here."

(Leave room and take Mr. Form with you.)

Instructions for Newman's Inner Self

(You are the inner self of Mr. Newman. Both you and Mr. Newman will come into the room when Mr. Form and his Inner Self leave. In the room you will read the material below

202

to Mr. Newman. *You will stand behind him,* and you will read very slowly and very distinctly. When you finish reading sit down. Mr. Form will enter.)

"My name is Ned Newman—N-E-W-M-A-N. I just started working in this company two weeks ago. My boss is Mr. Form, a pretty nice fellow. I have just punched my time card and I see a note on it from Mr. Form. It reads: 'Ned Newman, come in to see me as soon as you came in.' What can he want? What is it all about? I don't like this. It smells like trouble!

"My card reads 8:43. I am 13 minutes late. Can this be the reasons? No one else comes in on time. Everybody punches in late. There's Gene Smith punching in right now, and there's Herbert Zebra coming in through the door. It can't be that. The other fellows told me when I started coming in on time that no one came in before a quarter to nine. I'm only doing what the others are doing. I don't want them to think I am better than anyone else. After all, sometimes I do stay later than others. All you have to do is look at my time card and you can see I average more than eight hours a day.

"This is a pretty good job. I like it. The fellows are fine. So is Mr. Form. I'll go out and wash my hands and then I'll go into his office and see what it is all about. Oh, here comes Mr. Form. (Loud and clear:) *Hello! Mr. Form, I was just coming in to see you.*"

(Sit down, and get out of the way.)

Case 10

Director's Notes

This is a relatively complicated case, since two techniques are used: role reversal and the chain. The problem itself is very simple.

Some hints for the director may be helpful at this point.

The director should not talk too much. He should use gestures to give directions as much as possible. To stop action, slap hands twice. In giving directions, work rapidly and unobtrusively, so as not to affect the warmup too much. Verbal directions should be short, sharp, and clear. Avoid bossiness, but do be clear, emphatic and assured.

The whole group gets all the directions from the director. They are simple, and easily retained. They go as follows:

"Today we are going to experiment with two different roleplaying techniques. The first one is role-reversal, which means this: a John and a Bill will roleplay a situation which I shall describe in a moment—then John and Bill shall reverse roles, that is to say John will play the role of Bill and Bill will play the role of John, continuing from the same point that I stopped them. This technique has the advantage of helping whoever will play the roles of John and Bill to understand the two roles.

"The chain technique is something like role reversal, except that we will obtain different Johns and Bills from the group. We may start with John 1 and end up with John 5.

"This session should be lots of fun and can be confusing, so I shall try to start and stop you several times. Please keep an eye on me and follow my signals.

"Now, here is the problem. Bill is John's direct work supervisor. Bill's the boss. John is an employee. John has a problem: he wants to convince Bill of something. Bill is resistant. So, the problem is for John to try to convince Bill. Bill, on the other hand, wants to convince John. We now have the classic requirements for a conflict. Let us see how John and Bill can act out the problem. This is it:

"John drives a truck. He is dissatisfied with it. Why—we shall find out from the John we use. Bill understands John's point of view, but what is more, he knows that in life every-thing can't be just as one would like it to be, and so he must answer John's argument because John cannot have a new truck.

"The locale is Bill's office. Bill will be seated here and John will come in. He may be in a good mood and may want to discuss this issue among others; he may be pretty angry about the truck, and may have taken it up many times; he may make a big issue out of it—this is up to John. The same can be said about Bill: he may be relaxed and happy to talk to John; he may be busy; or angry himself. Again this will be up to Bill. Now, let me divide the room into Johns and Bills. We want one-half of the group to be Johns and the other half to be Bills. We shall actually divide the room into two groups physically if possible: the Johns on this side of the room (make gesture) and the Bills on this side (make gesture). Please decide which you are: John or Bill and go to the proper side of the room. (If you get too many Johns or Bills, try to get an approximate equalization. It is important that some members get up and move about: this helps to warm-up the group.)

"Now, I shall pick out two Johns and two Bills to start off things. One pair will go out of the room while the first pair roleplays. After the first pair have roleplayed, we shall call in the second pair. In this way we shall be able to compare how the two couples interpret the role. (At this point the director asks four people to stand up: two Johns and two Bills. Then, he should ask one Bill and one John to go out of the room. After they are out, he continues.)

"Bill, please sit down. You are in your office. When I give John the signal, you and he begin. John, are you ready? When I give you the signal, come in and begin. Remember, it is your problem to see if Bill will get you a new truck. You have to think of all the reasons you can give him for a new machine.

"Now, the rest of you should observe how John and Bill act. All of you will get a chance to play the roles today, and try to see who does the best job, and try to learn from the others how to play a good Bill and a good John. Two things more: try not to laugh or interrupt the scene. And, I shall stop the action many times by clapping my hands like this (clap hands twice) and as soon as I clap my hands stop immediately.

"All right John, go in to see Bill."

(Let the situation go on about three to five minutes, then clap hands twice.)

"Now, without any discussion, let's see how the other John and Bill can do. (Call in the other couple.)

"Bill, take your seat. You are in your office. In a moment your employee John will come in. John, are you ready? When I give you the signal, go into Bill's office, and see what you can get him to do about your truck. When I clap my hands once that means you stop talking, and I shall give you more information. When I clap my hands twice, it is the end of the scene. All right? Go in John."

(Let Bill and John continue until they are warmed up. This may take two or three minutes. Wait until they seem to be interacting strongly. Then, *quickly*, clap hands once, go to Bill and John and say) "Change places. Continue from this point. You (pointing to Bill) are now John, and you (pointing to John) are now Bill. Keep going." (Let them continue from this point about two minutes, then clap hands once and *gesture* they should change and continue. *Say nothing.* In this way you train the group to obey signals. Let them continue about one minute, then clap hands once again, and signal another change. Let the scene continue about a minute or so, then clap hands twice and have John and Bill sit down.)

At this point the director may lead a discussion about the

two sets of Johns and Bills. In leading discussion, the director *should give no opinions*. This is of the greatest importance: the director is a nonintervening discussion leader and not an authority.

After the discussion, say:

"Now, we shall try the Chain technique. We shall use only people who have not yet been on the stage. Let me number the Johns. You are 1, you are 2, you are 3, etc. And now, let me number the Bills. You are 1, you are 2, you are 3, etc. When I slap my hands once, the John and Bill on the stage stop talking. Then I will point to John 2 from the group, and he will go on the stage and continue the conversation with the same Bill on the stage. Then after a while I'll slap my hands once and the conversation stops, and then I'll point to Bill 2. In this way we shall all have a chance to participate. Now, will John 1 and Bill 1 go on the stage and begin the conversation."

(The director will permit the interactions to go on about 2 or 3 minutes, and then will clap his hands, and have John 2 come up, replacing John 1. After another minute or so, he claps his hands again, and mentions to Bill 2 to replace Bill 1. This continues until every John and Bill has had a chance to participate.)

After every person has participated, the leader directs a discussion.

Observation Guides

WHEN A GROUP MEETS for a number of sessions for
training purposes using roleplaying as a technique for improvement, the use of a rating sheet can be helpful. Such a
sheet can be used to inform any individual about the opinions
of others, and can also serve as a guide for discussion. The
sheet illustrated on page 211 represents a "universal" rating system which can be employed for many purposes. By changing
terms, this sheet can be made more specifically useful for any
particular group.

In the "Directions" facing page 211 can be found instructions sufficient for trainees. Some further elaboration may be
worthwhile. The reason for using the unusual format of a
circle and an underline is because frequently no one can tell
which of any two divergent methods is the better. For example,
we cannot say what is better—to be *firm* or to be *flexible*. The
right way depends on the situation. Therefore, by means of
this technique, the rater can indicate what he thinks is right—
by underlining, and what he saw—by circling. The difference
between the two ratings is the "error," the disparity between
what was observed and what was deemed correct.

After the ratings are made, and after any discussion, the
forms are to be given to the protagonist. By looking over
the ratings of the specific factors, by comparing opinions of the
members and by reading any comments which raters can make
on the back of these "Roleplaying Rating Sheets" the protagonist receives feedback material.

The information on these sheets can be transferred to the "Roleplaying Summary Chart."

On page 213 we have drawn a variety of sample curves to show what are some of the possible patterns on this chart. The curve for "stand" is rather flat, indicating little change from session to session. But for "control" we see a rapid change for the better. This individual, who averaged about 5 in his first session, has moved up to 1½ by the tenth session. The curve for "communication" is high over-all with some variations. A person reading this would be told that this is an area in which he does well. For "attitude" we see little change over the first four sessions and then a rapid rise, sustained over the next several sessions. But for "emphasis" we see a slow and gradual change. In terms of "relations," the curve drops slowly, indicating the change observed is in the wrong direction. The curve illustrated for "structure" shows first a drop, then a rise. For "procedure" there is a fast rise and an equally rapid drop, showing some progress which was not sustained. With respect to "rate," the individual does poorly all along.

Let us stop for a moment to discuss what the problem might be for "rate." The data above this grid show almost complete agreement that this trainee's pace is too *rapid*.

Now, if we look at the bottom grid we see that the "over-all" rating, from session to session, has improved from about 3½ (or average) to about 5½.

Were this the summary chart of any individual, he could think that while he was improved with respect to *control, attitude,* and *emphasis,* that he still has problems in terms of *relations, procedure* and *rate.*

While the terms should be self-descriptive, it may be wise, if this system is used, for the roleplaying director and his trainees to go over these forms and attempt to agree on their meanings so that some consistency is obtained. Usually, there is little difficulty in understanding.

LEADERSHIP RATING SHEET
DIRECTIONS

1. On each of the nine scales circle the dot that represents your opinion of what the leader *did*.

2. Also, underline the dot that represents your opinion of what the leader *should* have done.

3. If what he did and what he should have done are the same, then the same dot would be circled and underlined.

4. There is no "good" or "bad" end on the first nine scales. Whether one should be flexible or firm, etc., depends on the situation.

5. The difference between the circled and the underlined dot represents the "error" of that factor in that situation.

6. Circle one dot of the "Over-all rating" to indicate your general reaction to the roleplayer's effectiveness.

ROLEPLAYING RATING SHEET

Name_____Observer_____

Situation_____Date_____

_____

_____

				DIFFERENCE
STAND	Flexible	• • • O • • •	Firm	( )
CONTROL	Leader	• • • O • • •	Subordinate	( )
COMMUNICATION	Talk	• • • O • • •	Listen	( )
ATTITUDE	Tense	• • • O • • •	Relaxed	( )
EMPHASIS	Person	• • • O • • •	Problem	( )
RELATIONS	Friendly	• • • O • • •	Cold	( )
STRUCTURE	Formal	• • • O • • •	Informal	( )
PROCEDURE	Directive	• • • O • • •	Non-directive	( )
RATE	Rapid	• • • O • • •	Slow	( )

OVERALL RATING

Poor   • • • O • • •   Good

ROLEPLAYING SUMMARY CHART
DIRECTIONS

1. This chart is your "report card" and tells you how you are doing and how you are developing in terms of the various factors and in terms of your over-all ratings.

2. Take all the "Roleplaying Rating Sheets" on you for any session or situation and count the number of times you were rated "too flexible" (circles to the left of underlines). Put this number in the space after "flexible" at the top of the grid labeled "stand" on the "Roleplaying Summary Chart."

3. Now count the number of times you were rated "too firm" (circles to the right of underlines). Put this number after "firm."

4. Count the cases where the circles and underlines coincide and put this number after "O.K."

5. Do the same for the other grids.

6. When rated again do the same, putting new numbers after the old ones as shown in the example on the opposite page.

7. Subtract the differences between the circles and underlines (maximum difference is 6) and record the numbers on the "Roleplaying Rating Sheets" for all factors.

8. For each factor, add these differences. Sum the differences for each factor and then divide by the number of raters. This number represents your "average error."

9. Place data on the grid of the "Roleplaying Summary Chart" in terms of the session and the "average error" as shown in the example on the facing page.

10. For "Over-all Rating" merely add the ratings, from 1 to 7 (poor=1, good=7) and average from the Rating Chart and transfer the averages to the Summary Chart.

ROLEPLAYING SUMMARY CHART

NAME *Walt Logan*

STAND

Flexible _0110000100_
Firm _6756876796_
OK _2113102102_

```
   1 2 3 4 5 6 7 8 9 10
0
1
2
3
4
5
6
```

CONTROL

Leader _____
Subordinate _____
OK _____

```
   1 2 3 4 5 6 7 8 9 10
0
1
2
3
4
5
6
```

COMMUNICATION

Talked _____
Listened _____
OK _____

```
   1 2 3 4 5 6 7 8 9 10
                        0
                        1
                        2
                        3
                        4
                        5
                        6
```

ATTITUDE

Tense _____
Relaxed _____
OK _____

```
   1 2 3 4 5 6 7 8 9 10
0
1
2
3
4
5
6
```

EMPHASIS

Person _____
Problem _____
OK _____

```
   1 2 3 4 5 6 7 8 9 10
0
1
2
3
4
5
6
```

RELATIONS

Friendly _____
Cold _____
OK _____

```
   1 2 3 4 5 6 7 8 9 10
                        0
                        1
                        2
                        3
                        4
                        5
                        6
```

STRUCTURE

Formal _____
Informal _____
OK _____

```
0
1
2
3
4
5
6
   1 2 3 4 5 6 7 8 9 10
```

PROCEDURE

Directive _____
Non-directive _____
OK _____

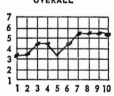

```
   1 2 3 4 5 6 7 8 9 10
```

RATE

Rapid _8857877867_
Slow _0001000000_
OK _0021101031_

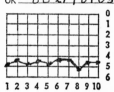

```
0
1
2
3
4
5
6
   1 2 3 4 5 6 7 8 9 10
```

OVERALL

```
7
6
5
4
3
2
1
   1 2 3 4 5 6 7 8 9 10
```

Definitions

Alter ego. An auxiliary ego who assumes the role of the "inner self" of the protagonist. A term used in psychodramatic roleplaying.

Antagonist. An individual who interacts with the protagonist or main character in any roleplaying situation.

Audience analyst. A member of a group who ordinarily does not participate during a session but who observes how the whole group participates and interacts. Ordinarily, he reports the progress of the group at stated intervals; usually at the end of subsections of sessions.

Auxiliary ego. A term used in psychodrama. The equivalent of antagonist. An assistant who interacts with a protagonist under the direction of the psychodramatic director.

Behind-the-back. A form of group therapy in which the protagonist retires from the group, with his back to the rest of the members who now discuss him while he is out of the "room" psychologically although in the room physically.

Director. The general name for the individual in charge of the production of roleplaying. He usually runs the session, obtains volunteers, selects antagonists, develops the situation, controls interaction by starting and stopping roleplaying, determines the employment of various techniques, and leads discussions. He may be totally unsophisticated in the particular problem of the individuals or groups, and so may serve as a technical director without involving himself in the content. Also known as leader, etc.

Empathy. The amount of understanding of another person's con-

214

cepts; the degree to which one can comprehend another's feelings and thinking without actually sharing them oneself.

Enactment. The actual playing of roles.

Extemporaneous roleplaying. Roleplaying which depends on the participants' playing without considerable preparation. Usually, participants are given general instructions and asked to participate without much prior rehearsal.

Group Psychotherapy. A form of mental treatment in which a number of patients meet with a therapist for the purpose of achieving desirable personality changes. Some forms of group psychotherapy employ psychodrama as a technique.

IDEAS technique. A procedure for conference leadership which includes the sequence of *Introduction, Demonstration* (via roleplaying), *Exercise* (which may include multiple roleplaying, buzz groups, etc. on the parts of the conferees, *Action,* or demonstrations from the floor, and *Summary* by the conference leader.

Imitation technique. A procedure in which B re-enacts the role of A as A played it. A then sees himself as in a mirror. Also called mirror technique.

In situ. On the spot.

Intensive Industrial roleplaying. A form of roleplaying quite similar to group psychotherapy designed to affect emotional attitudes at a deeper level than ordinary industrial roleplaying.

Monodrama. Roleplaying which involves one person who may interact with an imaginary antagonist, or in the split-monodrama may himself take both roles.

Multiple roleplaying. The simultaneous playing of the same situation by two or more groups. Thus if problem III is played by two or more sets of individuals at the same time, this is multiple roleplaying.

Observation guides. These are forms used for directed observations and evaluations of situations, or which may be prepared for specific situations, designed to help observers observe particular kinds of behavior and to evaluate them. In some guides, observers rate the adequacy of the observed behavior. They also serve to systematize discussions. Also known as guides.

Phasing. The over-all planning of a meeting so that it will run through various phases.

Play back. The replaying of a situation by means of some mechanical recording system. Usually tape recorders are used for playing back situations or parts of situations for more detailed analysis.

Protagonist. The "hero" or "chief character" in any roleplaying situation who contends with or against other individuals known as antagonists.

Psychodrama. Roleplaying when used for psychotherapeutic purposes.

Roleplaying (also spelled role playing, role-playing). Any of a variety of action techniques which involve people acting human relations situations in a realistic manner, under contrived (non-veridical) settings. Differentiated from the concepts of theatrical roleplaying where the acting is nonspontaneous but under contrived settings, and from sociological or real-life roleplaying where the action is spontaneous but under veridical circumstances.

Role-reversals. A procedure in which people switch roles either during the enactment of a situation or at the end. If A plays the role of a shopper and B plays the role of the saleswoman, and if during the course of the situation the director asks A now to play the role of the saleswoman and B the role of the shopper, the roles are switched or reversed. Some times known as role switching.

Round robin comments. A procedure in which every member of an observing group is asked in sequence to make comments about a particular phase or aspect of the observed interactions or behavior of individuals or subgroups.

Sensitivity training. Training for greater empathic understanding of other people. Although not limited to roleplaying, it has been mostly associated with this form of training.

Skit. A completely structured form of roleplaying in which the participants read their comments. Skits are generally created for the purpose of imparting information to the audience, and are usually structured in such manner as to convey a single point. A radio or television show where the actors read off their lines, or have memorized them, is an example of an entertainment skit.

Sociodrama. Roleplaying when used for the purpose of instruction of the audience. The role players themselves need not be affected by the behavior, and may be professional actors, etc.

Sociometry. A method for measuring the feeling interaction patterns of individuals to other members of any group, resulting in a sociometric map which consists of lines of preferred relationships between individuals. From such sociometric maps one can determine the stars or major individuals in the groups, cliques, isolates, etc.

Split-monodrama. Roleplaying in which one person simultaneously takes two or more roles, as for example acting the parts of a foreman and employee.

Spontaneity. A term introduced by J. L. Moreno, Viennese born psychiatrist, to represent the main purpose of psychotherapeutic roleplaying or psychodrama. Spontaneity refers to "the ability to respond adequately to a new situation or to respond in a new and adequate way to an old situation."

Structured roleplaying. Structuring refers to the degree of prior instruction given participants. Structuring can vary from almost none when a protagonist creates a problem to almost complete when a skit is enacted.

Substitute roleplaying. In this procedure one person assumes the real-life role of another person for a limited time principally in order to understand the position of the other, or perhaps to demonstrate to the other how the role might be played in real life. An example would be if A, who is B's superior, assumes B's role in real life while B watches on, in order for A to understand B's problems or for B to understand how A would handle his position.

Value analysis. A system of identifying and analyzing important variables in roleplaying. Observation guides are usually used in value analyses.

Warm up. The process of getting a group to loosen up and become ready to work. There are many techniques for this purpose including lectures, buzz groups, audience questions, etc.

APPENDIX IV

Annotated Bibliography

1. ANONYMOUS. Industrial psychology pays in this plant. *Dun's Review & Modern Industry*, 1948, 16, 67-68.

Dr. Alfred J. Marrow, a psychologist and president of the Harwood Corporation, uses modern psychological techniques in running his company. Examples are given of how roleplaying is used for the purpose of better communications and problem-solving.

2. ANONYMOUS. Act it, learn it. *Business Week*, April 9, 1949, 96-103.

Roleplaying, form of "let's pretend" uses no script and has no rehearsals. To improve social skills, foremen need lots of practice, which roleplaying can provide. The American Type Founders Co. is one of the first organizations to have used industrial roleplaying. The general phases are: (1) foremen meet to set up principles of behavior, (2) a foreman-in-training is briefed on a sample problem, (3) two workers meet this foreman and act out the problem, (4) recordings are made, and (5) there is a post-roleplaying discussion session.

3. ANONYMOUS. Acting that teaches how to handle people. *Dun's Review & Modern Industry*, 1949, 17, 50-52.

Roleplaying has long been used as a demonstration and training method in sales development. Its value depends on the dictum that we learn best by actually doing. Everybody is aware of things he knows how to do but still cannot do them. In using roleplaying for training, the situation should be realistic, just hard enough to be difficult to solve. Roleplaying is a superior procedure for getting messages across and is much superior to written language for avoiding equivocality of meanings. Roleplaying has value in helping to understand how others think and feel which is the beginning of good morale in industrial leadership.

4. ANONYMOUS. Role playing pays off for Ethyl. *Sales Management,* 1953, (Nov. 10), 71, 41.
Salesmen at the Ethyl Corporation were trained by playing roles which were recorded and then played back.

5. ANONYMOUS. Role playing in training supervisors. *Factory Management and Maintenance,* 1954, 112, 102-105.
This article contains a summary and analysis of 107 replies to a questionnaire about industrial roleplaying originally sent to 445 training directors.

6. ANONYMOUS. 64 hints to help you make role playing work. *Factory Management and Maintenance,* 1954 (Jan.), 112, 282-290.
These 64 hints come from comments made on a questionnaire returned by 107 training directors who use roleplaying. Samples: (1) Give participant a full understanding of what they are going to do; (64) Help players to save face.

7. ANONYMOUS. Role playing. *Industrial Distribution,* Sept. 1957, 113-136.
Roleplaying in sales training accomplishes these purposes: Reality testing by using true-to-life situations; Learning, by doing; seeing another's point of view; handling problems on the spot; solving problems through people; obtaining full participation; and affecting attitudes. Roleplaying is used to (1) teach fundamentals, (2) for specific sales problems, (3) for sales problems within company, (4) for phone and counter salesmen, (5) sales supervisor training, (6) general skill practice, and (7) practice in human relations skills. Pitfalls and booby traps in directing roleplaying are discussed.

8. ARGYRIS, C. Role playing in action. *New York State School of Industrial and Labor Relations, Cornell University.* Bulletin No. 16, May, 1951.
Argyris covers the general purposes of roleplaying, including a definition, where it can be used; a point of view about its value, and why roleplaying is valuable in re-education; how to prepare for roleplaying, including getting problems out on the table, and getting the members to want to experience a change; how to define the skit and roleplaying, how to help the group to observe, evaluating roleplaying and replaying roles. The last section contains suggestions for the practical use of roleplaying as a training technique and covers the areas of resistance, and gives a number of hints to the director about roleplaying procedures.

9. BARRON, MARY E. Role practice in interview training. *Sociatry,* 1947, 1, 198-208.
Roleplaying can be used for the effective transference of principles into methods. Because the interview is a kind of unrehearsed play between two persons, psychodramatic or roleplaying methods are particularly appropriate in training interviewers. After a practice session, trainees evaluate an interview, and then practice themselves.

10. BAVELAS, A. Role playing and management training. *Sociatry,* 1947, 1, 183-191.
This is a pioneer article about roleplaying in industrial use. Bavelas suggests a procedure with 14 steps.
    1. Short discussion of problem area.
    2. 2 protagonists (leaders) removed from group (X and Y).
    3. Problem to be played is described by the leader.
    4. A "worker" is selected from remaining group.
    5. The "worker" is prepared for his role.
    6. Props are set.
    7. Call in one protagonist and give him instructions.
    8. Leader stops session when indicated.
    9. X returns to group and becomes an observer.
    10. Y is now called in and interacts with "worker."
    11. Leader summarizes.
    12. X and Y are asked for their reactions; also the "worker."
    13. Group has general discussion.
    14. A new member (Z) is asked to replay the leader role.

11. BECKHARD, R. Role playing: Do it yourself technique. *Sales Management,* 1956 (Apr. 1), 76, 27-29.
Instructions are given for using roleplaying in the training of salesmen with general do's and don'ts.

12. BLANSFIELD, M. G. Consider "value analysis" to get the most out of role playing. *Personnel Journal,* 1953, 34, 251-254.
Roleplaying can be relatively ineffective unless "value analysis" is used. Some system of identifying and rating important variables of roleplaying should be used. On the basis of experience with training groups, the author found 15 areas useful for evaluation.

13. BLANSFIELD, M. G. Role playing as a method in executive development. *Journal of Personnel Administration and Industrial Relations,* 1954, 1, 131-135.
Roleplaying has three major purposes: changing of behavior, giving of information, and the learning of techniques for problem-solving.

14. BLANSFIELD, M. G. Role Playing: A suggested method of introduction to training groups. *Journal of the American Society of Training Directors*, 1957, 11 (1), 19-22 *passim*.

Resistance to roleplaying is usually based on insecurity or the fear of ridicule. However, the stress and tension of participation is an aid to learning if handled properly. The writer suggests these rules:
1. Don't formalize and frighten.
2. Avoid terms as "roleplaying" and "psychodrama."
3. Get group relaxed, and don't force roleplaying.
4. Avoid too many preliminaries.
5. Use Multiple Role Playing first, getting whole group to work in pairs.
6. Use a written problem.
7. Use team observers.
8. Use buzz groups for discussions.

15. BOGUSLAW, R. & BACH, G. R. "Work culture management" in industry: a role for the social science consultant. *Group Psychotherapy*, 1959, 12, 134-142.

The special conditions of a formally organized work environment and the objectives and operations of social science consultants working within these industrial frameworks are discussed. Through the use of roleplaying techniques, work group members are given an opportunity to understand and discuss the inadequacies of their previous behavior. Roleplaying is more effective when the group includes members familiar with the definitions of the appropriate goals, roles, and activities for the group.

16. BORGATTA, E. F. Analysis of social interaction: Actual, role playing and projective. *Journal of Abnormal and Social Psychology*, 1956, 40, 190-196.

A group of subjects were evaluated in terms of actual behavior, roleplaying behavior and pencil and paper tests. When relationships between the three situations were analyzed, it appeared that predictions from tests to actual or roleplaying behavior were weak, and that considerable caution should be exercised in attempting to predict from verbal to action behavior. On the other hand roleplaying appeared to give the same kind of information that was obtained from observations of unrehearsed actual behavior.

17. BRADFORD, L. P. Supervisory training as a diagnostic instrument. *Personnel Administration*, 1945, 8, 3-7.

Supervisory training necessarily contains diagnosis. Using roleplaying as an auxiliary method, the author found that because acting is spontaneous, attitudes are revealed. Techniques of handling problems are well illustrated in this manner. Participants tend to choose problems meaningful for them.

18. BRADFORD, L. P. & LIPPITT, R. Role playing in supervisory training. *Personnel,* 1946, 27, 358-369.

> While training in industry has been remarkably successful in affecting work skills, it has been unsuccessful in changing the human relations ability of supervisors. ". . . . exhortations will never transmit the finger dexterity essential to operate a typewriter but we evidently feel a foreman can be taught to handle situations . . ." A protocol of a typical training session is given. The roleplaying director's skill depends on his ability to make good selections of scenes, setting of the scenes to develop what is important, knowing when to cut off action, and ability in leading post-roleplaying discussion.

19. BROADED, C. H. A statement of the practical application of role playing as a training device. *Sociometry,* 1951, 14, 69-70.

> Roleplaying supplemented by "how to" material is superior to a procedure which concerns itself only with human relations interactions.

20. BRONFENBRENNER, U. & NEWCOMB, T. M. Improvisations—an application of psychodrama in personality diagnosis. *Sociatry,* 1948, 1, 367-382.

> A discussion of the use of roleplaying for testing as used by the Office of Strategic Services during World War II. In addition to judging participants, judges were themselves also judged for capacity to evaluate others. The "cases" or "plots" were modified in many cases to suit individuals, being tailor-made for their personalities and individualities. Similar procedures were used in a study to predict successful clinical psychologists for the Veterans Administration. In testing, verbal content, character of voice, and bodily movements were considered important variables. A standard set of six common human conflict situations is also outlined.

21. BURNS, R. K. & CORSINI, R. J. The IDEAS technique. *Group Psychotherapy.*

> The IDEAS technique has five parts: I—The Introduction in which the conference leader lectures on the problem; D—a roleplaying Demonstration by trained assistants, or members of the group; E—and Enactment by members via multiple roleplaying; A—action, or the demonstration to the group by subgroups of what they have done; and S—Summary, the leader's final integration of the session.

22. CALHOON, R. P. Role playing as a technique for business. *Michigan Business Review,* 1950, 2(6), 29-32.

> Roleplaying has been used semiformally for sales training for many years. Among its values revealing how lines of reasoning sound in practice, anticipation of problems, helping to make timing more

effective, etc. Roleplaying attacks the problem of attitudes more directly than any other method. Among its advantages are that it uses down-to-earth situations, helps to develop practical solutions, and brings out weaknesses in any human relations problem.

23. COHEN, J. The technique of role-reversal: a preliminary note. *Occupational Psychology*, 1951, 25, 64-66.

Role-reversal is a technique which helps A decide whether B really understands him and which helps B learn whether he can restate A's propositions to A's satisfaction. The author claims that "the effort to understand is the beginning of reconciliation" and recommends role-reversal for such purposes.

24. CORSINI, R. J. The role playing technique in business and industry. *Chicago: Industrial Relations Center.* Occasional Paper No. 9, April 1957.

Roleplaying has three major uses: diagnostic, training, and instructing. There are a variety of procedures available which call for a sensitive well-trained leader for success. Some procedures and typical cases illustrated.

25. CORSINI, R. J. Role playing: its use in industry. *Advanced Management*, 1960, 25, (2), 20-23.

Roleplaying has three primary functions: to train (by experiencing); to instruct (via observation); and to evaluate (through critical observations). Its essential value lies in the simultaneous use of the three primary modalities of action, thought, and emotion, which makes a roleplaying situation holistic, spontaneous, and natural. A case example of the use of roleplaying in training of an executive is cited.

26. CORSINI, R. J. & HOWARD, D. D. Training through role playing. *Concept*, 1960, 2(1), 43-46.

Roleplaying permits participants to practice reality, thus helping them to attain higher levels of on-the-job functioning through self-criticism and comments by others which increase a person's awareness.

27. CORSINI, R. J. & PUTZEY, L. J. Bibliography of group psychotherapy. Beacon, N. Y.: Beacon House, 1957.

A bibliography of approximately 1700 items about group psychotherapy, including several hundred about psychotherapeutic roleplaying (psychodrama). A number of articles about group procedures in industry are indexed.

28. FANTEL, E. Psychodrama in the counseling of industrial personnel. *Sociatry*, 1948, 2, 384-398.

Roleplaying was used in an industrial situation where management-employee tensions were present. By acting out various situations, better understanding of the personalities of three salesmen were determined, and a clearer understanding of the problems involved was obtained.

29. FOLEY, A. W. Extemporaneous role playing: its several advantages. *Personnel Journal,* 1955, 34, 177-180.

Extemporaneous roleplaying is described as situations written on cards, given to subjects to read for one minute and then to be acted out for two-three minutes, has some advantages over "rehearsed" roleplaying which tends to be superficial and artificial. After the roleplaying, short discussions are held. This method is valuable in warming up a new group.

30. FRANKS, T. W. A note on role playing in an industrial setting. *Group Psychotherapy,* 1952, 5, (59), 63.

A description is given of the use of roleplaying in an industrial problem which revolved about poor communication and ineffective managing techniques. Attitudinal changes occurred rapidly which led to better relationships.

31. FRANKS, T. W. Project-centered group treatment. *Group Psychotherapy,* 1959, 12, 161-165.

A case history of an industrial problem having to do with morale is recounted. First, out of a plant population of 1000 employees, a total of 120 were located who were natural leaders by asking employees 'Who you think I should talk to . . . ?" These 120 people were formed into 12 groups of ten each. Each group met weekly. Care was taken to have a heterogeneous grouping. At the end of the sessions, in each of the ten groups a decision was made to accept a plan previously rejected by the employees, which had been the original purpose of the meeting. Roleplaying was used during the sessions to point out how the plan would work.

32. FRENCH, J. R. P. Retraining an autocratic leader. *Journal of Abnormal and Social Psychology,* 1944, 39, 224-237.

A discussion of the retraining of an ineffective, autocratic leader of a boy-scoutmaster training program. Through roleplaying before a group of other leaders and by means of discussions, this formerly dull and rigid trainer became more flexible. A protocol of a session is given in illustration.

33. FRENCH, J. R. P. Role playing as a method of training foremen. *Sociometry,* 1945, 8, 410-422.

Stenographic notes of the handling of an actual problem in foremen training are presented in this article. Roleplaying's advantages for industrial training is that it is flexible, realistic, stimulates participation, involvement, and identification. It helps trainees by providing concrete realistic situations, enables the trainer to give immediate coaching, permits diagnostic observations, and leads to sensitivity training.

34. GORDON, M. Role playing in industry. *Group Psychotherapy,* 1959, 12, 187-191 (reprinted from *The Wall Street Journal,* March 15, 1957).

One way to obtain insight into situations is to roleplay the parts. A case is cited of an advertising supervisor who sold newspapers on a street corner in order to understand consumers' reactions to a particular newspaper. A number of instances of use of this and the more conventional kinds of roleplaying are given in support of the thesis that roleplaying can play an effective part in business and industry.

35. GORDON, R. M. Interesting modifications on role playing. *Journal of the American Society of Training Directors,* 1956, 10 (5), 25-29, *passim.*

Two basic principles of effective teaching are practice and participation. Roleplaying, of all techniques, comes closest to satisfying these demands. The author suggests two variations of Multiple Role Playing, called Group Role Playing and Group Multiple Role Playing. In the latter version, the following steps are taken:
1. Different roles are assigned to members.
2. The characters are grouped and discuss their roles.
3. They then act out in role groups.
4. There is discussion by characters.
5. Leader summarizes but does not comment.

36. HAIRE, M. Industrial Social Psychology In Gardner Lindzey, (Ed.), *Handbook of Social Psychology.* Vol. II. Cambridge, Mass.: Addison-Wesley Pub. Co., 1954, 1104-1123.

In a short section on page 1116, Haire states that roleplaying has offered a promise of theoretic analysis of roles, their meaning in groups, and a research tool for investigation of group structure and the role of the individual in the group. In practice neither of these have been realized. Roleplaying has chiefly been a very practical device for accomplishing the particular function of training supervisors.

37. HARDT, E. New York City Workshops successful. *The Journal of Industrial Training,* 1952, 6 (1), 18-20.

This is a summary report of a workshop of the National Association of Training Directors devoted to roleplaying. A number of speakers discussed the theory, applications, uses, values, and dangers of this action procedure in industrial use.

38. HUFFMAN, H. The play's the thing. *Business Education World,* 1948, 26, 392-395.

The use of skits in business education training is discussed.

39. JACKSON, T. A. Role playing in supervisor development. *Journal of Industrial Training,* 1951, 5 (2), 6-9, *passim.*

Industrial training procedures have developed from those where the trainees were passive auditors to those which require greater participation. Roleplaying is a fourth-stage development which maximizes practicing applications of principles of good human relationships. While it is potentially the most valuable training procedure, much depends on the skill of the trainer. Roleplaying deals primarily with the manner in which things are done. It can reveal to people what they are doing, leading to personal insights which precede personal changes.

40. KAULL, J. L. Combining role playing, case study and incident method for human relations training. *Journal of American Training Directors,* 1954, 8, 16-19.

Traditional lecture methods were found not effective in helping supervisors change behavior, and so roleplaying was tried. The author reports: ". . . . follow-through sessions proved exceptionally valuable in demonstrating to first-line supervisors the possible consequences of their behavior."

41. KELLOGG, E. E. A role playing case: how to get the most out of it. *Personnel Journal,* 1954, 33, 179-183.

Practical suggestions for using roleplaying in foremen training, especially techniques for getting such individuals to accept this procedure as a legitimate and worth-while method of learning, are given.

42. KLEIN, A. F. *Role playing in leadership training and group problem solving.* New York: Association Press, 1956.

A text for employing group procedures involving roleplaying. Suited for people interested in becoming conference leaders. It is oriented to practical use.

43. LAWSHE, C. H., BRUNE, R. L. & BOLDA, R. A. What supervisors say about role playing. *Journal of the American Society of Training Directors,* 1958, 12, (8), 3-7.

Forty-five management trainees in three groups where roleplaying was used, were asked on the fifth session to indicate their attitudes to this procedure, to test the idea that foremen are naturally resistant to this method. Results were uniformly favorable to the idea that roleplaying is acceptable to such individuals. For example 75% said "no" to the question "Does roleplaying put you on a spot?" To the question "Do you have to be a born actor to do a good job of roleplaying?" 95% said "no." 89% said "yes" to the question "Does roleplaying make a problem easier to understand?" 91% disagreed with the contention that roleplaying is more of a game than a training technique; and more people stated they would rather be the foreman (protagonist) (55%), than the employee roleplayer (antagonist (32%), while only 9% said they would prefer merely to be onlookers. The writers conclude that roleplaying does not automatically encounter resistance.

44. LIPPITT, R. The psychodrama in leadership training. *Sociometry,* 1943, 6, 286-292.

Roleplaying has these advantages in industrial training: it gives the trainer an opportunity to observe the trainee in action and to diagnose his real-life leadership style; enables him to focus on the leadership problems of the trainee; makes it possible for a number of trainees to profit at the same time; creates an atmosphere of objectivity; makes it possible to practice new leadership styles and perfect their execution; and show how it is possible to anticipate and handle new situations.

45. LIVERIGHT, A. A. Role playing in leadership training. *Personnel Journal,* 1951, 29, 412-416.

Roleplaying has been in use in unions for training union delegates how to handle grievance procedures. It is valuable to demonstrate how a problem can be handled. Six steps are described: (1) choosing a problem, (2) agreeing on details, (3) defining the roles of the players, (4) defining the roles of the spectators, (5) the roleplaying itself, and (6) postsession discussion.

46. LIVERIGHT, A. A. Skits in leadership training. *Personnel Journal,* 1951, 30, 64-66.

Skits are structured situations played before a group with a purpose of illustrating a problem and obtaining discussion. They are not used primarily for the purpose of personal development.

47. LONERGAN, W. G. Role playing in an industrial conflict. *Group Psychotherapy,* 1957, 10, 105-110.

Lonergan reports how roleplaying was used to effect communication in a strike situation. Management was unable to change the attitudes of foremen with reference to moving certain materials because the foremen felt that the striking employees would regard the move as hostile. When management roleplayed a board meeting to show their position, the observing foremen finally understood the import of the various points of view, and changed their own opinions.

227

48. LONERGAN, W. G. Management trainees evaluate role playing. *Journal of the American Society of Training Directors,* 1958, 12 (10), 20-25.

This paper reports the reactions of 25 management trainees to roleplaying. 78 per cent of the comments to ten groups of questions were judged to be favorable to roleplaying.

49. MACHAVER, W. V. & FISCHER, F. E. The leader's role in role playing. *Journal of Industrial Training,* 1953, 7, 6-16.

Roleplaying not only is of value to direct participants but also to onlookers. The leader of a session has executive decisions to make with regard to controlling scenes. The leader must be careful not to use roleplaying to put across a prepared message, but should permit members to be spontaneous. Recorders and playback are advisable in industrial use.

50. MAIER, N. R. F. Dramatized case material as a springboard for role playing. *Group Psychotherapy,* 1953, 6, 30-42.

Roleplaying is valuable for sensitizing persons to feeling of others, and for developing listening and empathy skills. However, there is frequently resistance to this procedure. A new method of dramatized skits to be read by participants is suggested as a procedure for reducing tensions, and as leading to more spontaneous dramatizations of problems.

51. MAIER, N. R. F. & SOLEM, A. R. Audience Role Playing: a new method in human relations training. *Human Relations,* 1951, 4, 279-294.

In ARP the audience is asked to react to an attitude questionnaire, then given a lecture designed to change attitudes. Then another attitude sampling is made. Then, roleplaying is done on a related issue, and a further recheck of attitudes is made. Generally, roleplaying seems to be much more effective in changing attitudes than are lectures.

52. MAIER, N. R. F., SOLEM, A. R., MAIER, A. A. *Supervisory and executive development.* New York: John Wiley and Sons, 1957.

This book contains a short introduction to the use of case material in roleplaying, and 20 structured situations, of the single and multiple type, referring to individual and group problems.

53. MAIER, N. R. F. & ZERFOSS, L. F. MRP: a technique for training large groups of supervisors and its potential use in social research. *Human Relations,* 1952, 5, 177-186.

MRP is a combination of the Phillips 66 "buzz group" procedure and roleplaying. It is designed to be used with large groups, which are to be broken into smaller groups who will then roleplay simultaneously a described situation. A typical problem with the roles of the individual members is given in illustration.

54. MARROW, A. J. Group meetings pay off. *Business Week,* 1950, (May) 20, 82-91.
This is an interview with Dr. Marrow, a psychologist and president of Harwood Manufacturing Company with reference to his ideas of dealing with employees. He advocates democratic, group-centered methods, and uses roleplaying for illustrating and training.

55. MASSELL, M. Setting the training stage for better conferences. *American Business,* 1949, (March) 19, 14-15.
The case history method of training indicates the *what* but not the *why* nor the *how*. Some minor matters may be of great importance in human relations, and roleplaying can point them out. Roleplaying is a good procedure for initiating discussions. The author indicates how roleplaying can be used for demonstration and how the leader can then make comments and lead discussion.

56. MAYER, J. & PLUTCHIK, R. Group coaching as an adjunct to role playing in human relations training. *Journal of the American Society of Training Directors,* 1957, 11(5), 44-45.
Three major principles should be used in human relations training: give participants as much involvement as possible, maintain interest, and relate material to "real life" situations. The writers describe a procedure, stated to be superior to multiple roleplaying which has the following steps:
  1. Written roles are prepared for typical problems.
  2. Roleplayers to discuss problem in teams of two. Several sets of roleplayers may be used.
  3. Director and group discuss the situation and what to look for.
  4. Teams are called in and interviewed by group resolutions.
  5. Group coaches the roleplayers.
  6. After demonstrations, there is discussion.

57. MEYER, A. Spontaneity. *Sociometry,* 4, 150-167.
A concentrated discussion of the theoretical aspects of spontaneity as applied to roleplaying.

58. MILLER, D. C. Introductory demonstrations and applications of three major uses of role playing for business and government administrators. *Sociometry,* 1951, 14, 45-58, 67-68.

Three uses of industrial roleplaying that can be demonstrated are: (1) conference techniques for problem solving, (2) techniques for employee selection, and (3) training methods for employers and supervisors. Miller gives 14 steps for illustrating the first, 13 for illustrating the second and 12 steps for illustrating the third method before large groups.

59. MILLER, D. C. A role playing workshop for business and government administrators: its research implications. *Group Psychotherapy*, 1953, 6, 50-62.

A detailed outline and summary of an intensive one-day workshop in industrial roleplaying directed at administrator problems is given with a discussion of research implications of roleplayng.

60. MOODY, K. A. Role playing as a training technique. *Journal of Industrial Training*, 1953, 7, 3-5.

Roleplaying can serve as a mirror in which participants can see themselves. It fosters insight and empathy. It makes intangible concepts concrete. Observing behavior is much more impressive than listening.

61. MORENO, J. L. & BORGATTA, E. F. An experiment with sociodrama and sociometry in industry. *Sociometry*, 1951, 14, 71-104.

This is a protocol of a session directed by Dr. Moreno in which industrial problems are elicited and one of them acted out on the psychodrama stage. The session is then analyzed sociometrically.

62. O'DONNELL, W. G. Role playing as a practical training technique. *Personnel*, 1952, 9, 275-289.

This is a concentrated summary of the uses, advantages, and limitations of roleplaying in industrial training. The author gives credit to George Herbert Mead for clarifying the importance of roleplaying in social psychology. Roleplaying permits the gap between principles and practice to be seen and then gapped. It is the proconstruction and reconstruction of experience. The article contains a number of practical hints for the most effective use of roleplaying in industrial situations.

63. O'DONNELL, W. G. Role playing in training and management development. *Journal of the American Society of Training Directors*, 1954, 8, 76-78.

"It (roleplaying) is learning by doing under conditions in which mistakes are much less costly to management than when made through on-the-job trial-and-error means of gaining experience in handling problems of human relations." "Roleplaying has its foundations firmly in the socio-psychological principle that all human behavior is roleplaying of some sort and that the essential character of social intelligence involves putting one's self in the place of

230

others." Roleplaying as well as other action methods of training are imbedded in a democratic concept that there should be a consistency between training method, individual and corporate needs.

64. PETERS, G. A. & GARDNER, S. Inducing creative productivity in industrial research scientists. *Group Psychotherapy,* 1959, 12, 178-186.

A special limited-goal program is indicated for research personnel in industry to help individuals develop their creative powers. A *creative-induction* program similar to intensive industrial roleplaying is indicated using roleplaying as a major technique. This program is not concerned so much with personality modifications but rather the induction of higher levels of creativity.

65. PETERS, G. A. & PHELAN, J. G. Practical Group Psychotherapy reduces supervisor's anxiety. *Personnel Journal,* 1957, 35, 376-378.

The authors contend that many industrial supervisors are in dire need of psychotherapeutic help. One method of meeting this need is to use group psychotherapy in the form of Intensive Industrial Role Playing, which is effective in changing the attitudes of supervisors.

They claim that "mere familiarity with a new role and experience in handling routine problems associated with new roles lessens the threatening quality of such new social adjustments."

66. PETERS, G. A. & PHELAN, J. G. Relieving personality conflicts by a kind of role playing. *Personnel Journal,* 1957, 36, 61-64.

The authors describe Intensive Industrial Role Playing, a form of group psychotherapy based on the notion the "knowledge of what is right does not ensure emotional acceptance nor the ability to put knowledge into action." There are four phases to this method: (1) Planning, including program orientation, individual interviews and mapping out procedures, (2) Group Interaction including the warm-up, ego involvement, content clarification, and feeling analysis, (3) Individual ventilation through periodic interview, suggested every six sessions, and (4) Group Interaction in terms of new sequences of six session.

The authors comment on "the saving in time for the group leader (or lowered costs to industry) in comparison to individual therapy since it . . . requires only 25% as much time . . ."

The roleplaying leader should provide general direction: his leadership should not be obvious; and he should never place himself in a teaching position.

67. PETERS, G. A. & PHELAN, J. G. Practical group psychotherapy and role playing for the industrial supervisor. *Group Psychotherapy,* 1959, 12, 143-147.

A fundamental problem in industry is to determine how to change the basic negative attitudes of industrial supervisors. This is an important problem because there is a direct relationship between the nature of the interpersonal relationships within a company and productivity and profits. *Intensive Industrial Role Playing* offers an economical remedy for improving problems involved in changing basic attitudes of industrial supervisors. Greater responsibility is placed upon the group leader in understanding the personality dynamics, assets, limitations, and needs of each individual for good group interaction.

68. PETERS, G. A. & PHELAN, J. G. Role Playing techniques in industrial situations. *Group Psychotherapy*, 1959, 12, 148-155.

Productivity depends more on psychological than on environmental factors. Psychological factors, to be optimal, depend greatly on proper communication and perceptions. But these depend basically on attitudes. To change attitudes in industry, a type of group psychotherapy using roleplaying is recommended. The format is that four roleplayers under the direct supervision of a leader interact while four other members serve as observers and commentators. Four phases are identified: (A) Planning, (B) Group Interaction, (C) Individual ventilation, and (D) Group interaction.

69. PHELAN, J. G. An adaptation of role playing techniques to sales training. *Journal of Retailing*, 1954, (Winter) 149, *passim.*

The best method for training in social skills is to watch others, do it yourself, discuss and evaluate differences, and then try again. Conferences do not permit trainees to get the feel of actually how to proceed when on the spot. Effective sales training using roleplaying depends on good planning and direction. A discussion is given of general procedures applicable in roleplaying sales training and evaluation interviews. The use of role reversal is discussed.

70. PLANTY, E. G. Training employees and managers. (*In* Planty, E. G., McCord, W. S., & Efferson, C. A., *Training employes and managers for production & teamwork*). Ronald, 1948, 183-186.

There is sometimes a discrepancy between apparent understanding and acceptance versus actual behavior on jobs. Roleplaying is a solution because one can project himself in a situation, can submit himself for critical evaluation, and can practice new procedures and methods. Roleplaying is the method which evokes the fullest activity in learning. The author distinguishes between roleplaying where one acts out a situation spontaneously and a demonstration in which actors show the observers the right and wrong ways to handle human relations problems.

232

71. Rubin, C. G. A statement on the practical application of role playing as a selection technique by the Seattle Civil Service Department. *Sociometry*, 1951, 14, 59-62.

The Seattle Civil Service is experimenting with roleplaying for personnel selection and has already used such tests for selecting police women, purchasing agents, and contract agents. These situations, called performance demonstrations, bring out qualities not readily discerned by interviews or written examinations. An example of a structured problem for police women is given together with a rating form which includes voice and speech, ability to present ideas, comprehension of problem, judgment, emotional stability, self-confidence, diplomacy, and co-operation.

72. Scher, J. M. Two disruptions of the communication zone: a discussion of action and role playing techniques. *Group Psychotherapy*, 1959, 12, 127-133.

Two types of organizational aberrations which result in a disruption of the communicative process within a hierarchical structure are discussed. *Communicatio retarda* is a process which lacks goal-intendedness and results in a situation where no action is achieved. *Communicatio multiplex* refers to a situation in which too much competing or unorganized information is being handled, and is characterized by a lack of leadership and ordered interaction. Both concepts are demonstrated by examples.

Roleplaying is useful in that it keeps the "communication zone" open and ordered. It clarifies the situation and leads to meaningful decision making.

73. Schmidhauser, H. B. You, too, can role play. *Journal of the American Society of Training Directors*, 1958, 12 (3), 2-11.

Roleplaying's value in business situations depend on these seven features: (1) others can observe situation, (2) participants learn by doing, (3) all quickly grasp essential conflicts, (4) conclusions, decisions and solutions can be arrived at, (5) participation fosters interest and motivation, (6) techniques elicit attitudes, and (7) beneficial co-operation is induced. Eleven terms found in roleplaying are defined. Some reports of successful use of this procedure are given.

74. Shaw, M. E. Role reversal. A special application of role playing. *Supervisory Development Today*, 1955.

Role reversal consists of having roleplayers change their positions or parts. It is used for producing insights, as a warm-up device, for developing the situation and for producing action. Among its various applications are to indicate how to handle grievances and for job instruction training. Examples of use are given together with a generalized procedure for the use of role reversal.

233

75. SHAW, M. E. Role playing—a procedural approach. *Journal of the American Society of Training Directors,* 1956, 10, (March-April), 23, *passim.*

Effective roleplaying depends on a procedural frame of reference which helps the leader meet ever changing needs of people in human relations training. Three phases are suggested: (1) the warmup, (2) the enactment, and (3) postsession analysis. Successful guidance of learning experience require that the leader accept that people are capable of solving the majority of their own problems and that a group's experience and understanding are superior to that of any other individual's, including the leader's.

76. SHAW, M. E. Training executives in action. *Group Psychotherapy,* 1956, 9, 63-68.

In view of some opinions that roleplaying might not be acceptable in industrial training, Shaw gives evidence that 79 per cent of 73 executives who enrolled in a communication course through the American Management Association accepted roleplaying without especial comment. A number of specific comments about this technique are cited in the article.

77. SHAW, M. E. Organizational considerations in role playing application. *Group Psychotherapy,* 1959, 12, 156-160.

Roleplaying in industry thus far has not yet been utilized to its potential. In most cases it has been used for fairly sterile didactic purposes, concerning itself with "methods," using "canned" situations, and in general not taking advantage of the enormous possibilities inherent in spontaneity roleplaying as employed in psychodrama. Shaw suggests that industry can use roleplaying in its more sensitive and powerful sense especially in the treatment of existing organizational groups in contrast to transient artificial training groups.

78. SPEROFF, B. J. Empathy and role-reversal as factors in industrial harmony. *The Journal of Social Psychology,* 1953, 37, 117-120.

Industrial conflict is provoked or mediated by intercommunication between disputing groups. Empathy serves the role of mediating good communication when defined as "the ability to put yourself in the other person's position." To establish empathy in disputes, when X expresses a point and Y disagrees, Y must present the point himself to X's satisfaction. This is an example of role-reversal, X taking Y's role, used to establish empathetic understanding.

79. SPEROFF, B. J. The group's role in role playing. *Journal of Industrial Training,* 1953, 7, 17-20.

Good roleplaying is group-centered. It has two major purposes: to allow a person to "feel the role of another" and to permit the player to reveal his true self. A number of specific techniques are described.

80. SPEROFF, B. J. Rotational role playing used to develop executives. *Personnel Journal,* 1954, 33, 49-50.

The author discusses the value of job rotation and interchange of roles for fuller development of individual executives and for increasing better understanding of problems of others.

81. SPEROFF, B. J. Scripts versus role playing. *Personnel Journal,* 1954, 32, 304-306.

Scripts are structured rules which roleplayers read. Their main purpose is to give information to the audience. While for many situations unstructured spontaneous dramas are superior, for other purposes scripts are better. In deciding which of the two to use, a great many factors have to be taken into consideration.

82. SPEROFF, B. J. Empathy and role-reversal as factors in communication. *Journal of Social Psychology,* 1955, 41, 163-165.

Role-reversal can be used to ensure good communication when the ordinary empathetic procedures do not work.

83. SPEROFF, B. J. Five uses of sound recordings of a group's role playing. *Personnel Journal,* 1956, 35, 50-51.

Five major uses of sound recordings in industrial roleplaying are:
1. Recordings of prior sessions can be the basis for a present group's discussion.
2. A session can serve as a model of a good interaction.
3. One can replay a session to have participants rehear what was said.
4. It is possible in this manner to compare different performances.
5. In this manner one can analyze, evaluate, or examine critically any "frozen" session.

84. SPEROFF, B. J. The "behind-the-back" way in training conference leaders. *Personnel Journal,* 1957, 35, 411-412, 435.

Speroff suggests the use of the "behind-the-back" technique in the training of industrial conference leaders. This method, calls for the trainee to interact with the group and then retire psychologically by turning his back to the group while they discuss him. This procedure, it is claimed, makes it easier for the group to discuss the "absent" individual since they are not inhibited by seeing him and makes it easier for him to listen to what is said since he is not emotionally upset by hearing critical material. Speroff claims per-

235

sonal insight, empathetic ability, and sensitivity to the feelings of others are developed by this method. More objective self-evaluations and greater skills in personal relations are fostered by this technique.

85. SPEROFF, B. J. Group therapy in industry: a case of intragroup conflict. *Group Psychotherapy*, 1957, 10, 3-9.

The author recounts a case study of a group of industrial employees whose relationships had degenerated progressively. By using a group therapy approach, including the use of roleplaying, in seven weeks the relationships were considerably improved.

86. SPEROFF, B. J. Role playing versus acting with scripts. *Nursing Outlook*, 1958, 3, 377-379.

In nursing training the use of scripts, which are completely structured interchanges, intended to show superior ways of dealing with hospital problems, are inferior to the more dynamic procedure of roleplaying to permit nurses to empathize with other people's feelings.

87. SPEROFF, B. J. Group psychotherapy as adjunct training in handling grievances. *Group Psychotherapy*, 1959, 12, 169-174.

A case history is cited to show how a labor relation staff was given training by means of a group therapy-like procedure aimed at improving their functioning. Individual problems were selected, roleplayed, and discussed. First, attention was paid to problems; later, to the individuals. As a result of a number of such sessions, the effectiveness of the supervisors increased, and they were able to handle almost twice as many cases as they had before.

88. STAHL, G. R. Role playing is ideal for training. *Sales Management*, 1953, (Nov. 10) 40, *passim*.

Shows how roleplaying can be used in the training of salesmen. This procedure is useful not only in improving skills, but also in changing attitudes. Twenty-four questions are asked and answered about roleplaying used for training.

89. STAHL, G. R. Training directors evaluate role playing. *Journal of Industrial Training*, 1953, 7, 21-29.

This is a summary of replies to questionnaires sent in 1951 and 1953 by training directors with reference to roleplaying in industry. The two major purposes of roleplaying are to develop skills and to change attitudes. A number of comments, favorable and unfavorable, sent in by training directors are reproduced.

90. STAHL, G. R. A statistical report of industry's experience with role playing. *Group Psychotherapy*, 1954, 6, 202-215.

Reports from 107 organizations regarding their reactions to role-playing are given. Generally, its two major purposes are: supervisor training and learning how to deal with specific problems. A number of specific attitudes are discussed in detail, together with statements of various commentators.

91. STANTON, H., BACK, C. W. & LITWAK, E. Role playing in survey research. *American Journal of Sociology*, 1956, 62, 172-175.

Survey data obtained through roleplaying may prove better than information obtained through interview procedures. Most subjects can roleplay, it is not difficult to train administrators to use this technique, and it yields information about the respondent under stress.

92. STARR, A. Role playing: an efficient technique at a business conference. *Group Psychotherapy*, 1959, 12, 166-168.

Roleplaying in a business conference can be an efficient technique for "putting points across." By having independent-from-the-organization people act out conflict situations, those on both sides of an issue can get to see the others' point of view.

93. STEINMETZ, C. Recordings help foremen improve industrial relations techniques. *Factory Management and Maintenance*, 1949, (Jan.) 107, 129-130.

A technique of human relations training using recording as a major method is described. Participants handle a structured case which is recorded. Later, the session is played back. The major participant gets a first chance to list and criticize his performance; then, others are permitted to evaluate it.

94. SYMONDS, P. Role playing as a diagnostic procedure in the selection of leaders. *Sociatry*, 1947, 1, 43-50.

The author analyzes 111 O.S.S. Improvisation situations. They fall into seven types: (1) Personal criticism—boss criticizes a worker, etc. (2) Interpersonal conflict—partnership dissolution, etc. (3) Moral issues—plagiarism, etc. (4) Interviews—hiring situations, etc. (5) Rejection situations—blackballing, etc. (6) Intrapersonal conflict—loyalty problems, etc. (7) Authority problems—reporting mutiny. These roleplaying situations can be used for the evaluation of personality, since different people handle such problems differently.

95. TAYLOR, J. W. Methods of increasing knowledge. *Journal of the American Society of Training Directors*, 1953, 7, 13-16, *passim*.

Training has three purposes: increasing knowledge, increasing skills, and improving attitudes. There are four ways of increasing knowledge: telling, showing, illustrating, and doing. A dozen ways

237

of increasing knowledge are listed: reading, lectures, etc., including roleplaying, defined simply as the case study method brought to life, utilizing the learning-by-doing principle. Roleplaying permits protected-from-penalty practice, pilot-running experimentation, creates new understanding, and convincingly, and is one of the most potent weapons in the training directors arsenal.

96. TUPES, E. C., CARP, A., & BORG, W. R. Performance in role playing situations as related to leadership and personality measures. *Sociometry*, 1958, 21, 165-179.

Three hypothesis were tested: (1) roleplaying scores are related to military officer effectiveness, (2) are related to other performance predictors, and (3) are related to personality scores rendered by peers. Based on over 200 USAF candidates, results indicate: nonchance relationships exist for the first hypothesis, but predictions are not efficient; significant relationships exist versus other performance tests; and significant relations exist between roleplaying scores and peer personality ratings. The authors believe that check lists of specific behaviors is a superior method of scoring roleplaying for evaluation.

97. TYLER, A. H. A case study of role playing. *Personnel*, 1948, 25, 136-142.

Roleplaying was first used in industrial training at the American Type Founders Company. This method has a number of advantages over other procedures including learning-by-doing; learning is put to immediate use; there is a competition to do better than others, etc. Sound recordings and playbacks are a main training tool. The conference leader who uses roleplaying has a very difficult task which calls for tact, patience, and understanding.

98. WEINLAND, J. D. Training interviews by the group method. *Journal of the American Society of Training Directors*, 1957, 11(2), 35-40.

The group training situation has some advantages over individual training for interviewers: criticism occurs without rancor; the group has a wide attention span and observes closely; there is a greater freedom of questioning; and individuals are helped to learn how to speak before groups. In the procedure used by the writer, students are interviewed in pairs in front of a class. The instructor also does demonstration interviewing. When special points are to be taken up, planned roleplaying is used.

99. WILKINSON, B. & MYERS, J. H. What good are role playing techniques? *Advanced Management*, 1954, 19, 23-24.

When roleplaying is not accepted, it is highly possible that the technique was misunderstood and misused. The authors applied

238

this procedure with success in a location where formerly it had not worked out well. They asked one-half of the group to identify with one and the other half to identify with the other person in two-person actions. The players had rehearsed the scene and purposely made errors. The group then discussed these errors. Sixteen questions are asked and answered by the authors.

100. WOLOZIN, H. Teaching personnel administration by role playing. *Personnel Journal,* 1948, 27, 107-109.

The author reports that he finds it much more satisfactory to teach personnel administration through roleplaying. He separates class groups into subgroups of six and has each group analyze and act out problem cases.

101. WYN-JONES, I. The significance of role playing. *Bacie Journal,* 1952, Jan.-Feb., 21-24.

Roleplaying is defined as "the physical interpretation of a mental pattern of behavior in a given situation." There is reason to doubt that whether this procedure has yet been used to its full advantage. Several types of roleplaying are described: dramatization of training based on a rehearsed script for demonstration purposes (information giving); spontaneous roleplaying where students' abilities to handle problems are tested (testing); roleplaying for insight through acting in a semistructured situation (training). Postsession analyses are regarded as important. Groups no larger than 15 are suggested for industrial roleplaying. Success depends in part on the attitudes of the students, and the ability of the instructor to create an air of reality about the situation.

102. ZANDER, A. F. Role playing: a technique for training a necessarily dominating leader. *Sociatry,* 1947, 1, 225-235.

In some situations, the leader must be dominating and should lead without consideration of the desires of those under his supervision. However, there are a variety of ways in which a necessarily dominating leader can secure better co-operation of subordinates. A condensed protocol is given of how this type of situation is handled. In a training course which meets for only a few sessions, the use of roleplaying brings up a number of problems, especially when unsympathetic individuals are in the group.

Professional and Training Organizations Through Which Roleplaying Training May Be Available

1. THE AMERICAN MANAGEMENT ASSOCIATION, 1515 Broadway, New York City, New York.

> This association conducts a variety of seminars and special institutes.

2. THE AMERICAN SOCIETY OF GROUP PSYCHOTHERAPY AND PSYCHODRAMA, 101 Park Avenue, New York City, New York.

> At annual meetings held in New York and elsewhere demonstrations of roleplaying are usually presented.

3. THE MORENO INSTITUTE, Beacon, New York.

> Here, several times annually, are held intensive institutes in therapeutic roleplaying.

4. THE INSTITUTE FOR GROUP PSYCHOTHERAPY, 430 North Bedford Drive, Beverly Hills, California.

> Special institutes in roleplaying techniques are held periodically for a variety of special purposes at this institute.

5. THE INDUSTRIAL RELATIONS CENTER OF THE UNIVERSITY OF CHICAGO, 975 East 60th Street, Chicago, Illinois.

> This center holds periodic conferences and institutes for special groups and purposes.

6. THE HUMAN RELATIONS TRAINING LABORATORY, DEPARTMENT OF PSYCHOLOGY, University of Texas, Austin, Texas.

Periodic institutes and training courses are given by this laboratory at which roleplaying is frequently featured.

7. DANIEL D. HOWARD ASSOCIATES, 28 East Jackson Blvd., Chicago 4, Illinois.

This management consulting firm conducts roleplaying institutes and training programs in industrial relations.

8. LEADERSHIP WORKSHOP, 30 Rockefeller Plaza, New York City, New York.

This organization specializes in action training techniques applied to 1st and 2nd level supervisors. Industrial groups meet for one week a Jug End Barn, Great Barrington, Massachusetts, and Onchiota Conference Center, Sterling Forest, New York.

Name Index

Subject Index